Favorite Pedal Tours
of Northern California

by Naomi Bloom

FINE EDGE
Productions
BISHOP, CALIFORNIA

Photos: All photos by Naomi Bloom except where noted
Cover photograph and preceding pages: Montara Lighthouse, San Mateo County Coast
Maps: Except where noted, originally appeared in *California Bicyclist*

Important Disclaimer

Any bicycle ride should be undertaken by responsible individuals. Cycling on public roadways and trails carries inherent risks. The authors, publishers, editors, distributors, retailers and others associated with this book are not responsible for errors or omissions and do not accept liability for any loss or damage incurred from using this book.

Table of Contents

Introduction

About nine years ago, when I was in charge of activities for Skyline Cycling Club, I received a flyer announcing an about-to-be-published magazine, *California Bicyclist*. The publisher, Michael Rosenberg, was contacting Bay Area bike clubs in search of advertisers, calendar listings, and freelance writers.

I called immediately and told him, "I have all three for you." He took my classified ad, told me where to send our club ride schedule, and invited me to send him some ride write-ups he could print as "Pedal Tours." I submitted three. He published two in the first issue, April 1983.

A week later Rosenberg called to say, "Of all the people who sent me articles, yours were the only ones I didn't have to completely rewrite. How would you like to do a monthly Pedal Tours column?"

The pay was next to nothing, but writing a monthly column about my favorite activity in the whole world was a labor of love.

Rosenberg has since retired, *California Bicyclist* has expanded into the Yellow Jersey Group of publications, and "Pedal Tours by Naomi Bloom" is no longer a monthly feature. But during eight years, from 1983 to 1991, I submitted more than 80 columns featuring some 140 bike rides.

Forty-four of those rides made the cut for this book. A good many are my personal favorites. More than a few were suggested by fellow members of Western Wheelers and Skyline Cycling Club. And a fair number have never before been published in any other bicycle touring book.

Of all my sources for route information, none has been more thorough than Grant Petersen's *Roads to Ride* and *Roads to Ride South*. I'm always delighted to quote a terse Petersen description, but I'm even happier to rely on his gradient calculations and mileages (much more accurate than any AAA map). For historical information, I most often turned to Carol O'Hare, author of *A Bicyclist's Guide to Bay Area History*.

I deserve no credit for the maps herein. The scrawls I submitted to the magazine were rendered into legibility by Howard Munson, and nearly all his efforts since mid-1986 are reproduced here. Those created before the advent of Yellow Jersey Art Director Janette Cavecche (all of which "disappeared" after publication) have been replicated electronically by Macintosh wizard Lorraine Schultz.

I owe heartfelt thanks for past and present support to my *California Bicyclist* editors — Michael Rosenberg, Shawn MacAndrew, and Kimberly Grob — all good friends as well as Pedal Tours fans. And to the Douglasses of Fine Edge Productions, especially Réanne for her thoughtful editorial suggestions. And finally to Sue Irwin, whose flying fingers quickly turned ASCII text into professional type.

Please join all of us in the joys of pedal touring in Northern California. See you on the road!

Naomi Bloom
Bishop, California
February 1992

Favorite Pedal Tours
of Northern California

Cycling the Sonomo County coastline offers absolutely magnificent scenery.

1. NORTH BAY
Sonoma, Napa, Marin Counties

Ask almost anyone to name the ideal venue for pedal touring. Your answer will most likely be...California wine country. But the country north of San Francisco Bay offers much more than vines and wines. Don't miss the rugged coastline's cliff-top views of crashing Pacific surf. Or the tough hills over coastal ridges to rustic dairylands. And remember to glimpse a chapter or two of California history. It's all here north of San Francisco Bay.

Two Days Riding the Cazadero Circuits
May 1988

These circuits originally appeared as "Scenic Rides Near the Sonoma County Coast."

Ever want to toss your bike on the car, pack a few things and steal away for a couple days? Nothing elaborate, just a weekend getaway from the same old roads and routines. An escape to some down-home atmosphere laced with long rides through the countryside or along the seaside.

Make that escape to Cazadero. A minimally organized scattering of summer homes and working ranches, Cazadero hugs the shores of Austin Creek about 20 miles northwest of Santa Rosa. It's part of the Russian River community, but there's none of the glitz and tourist traps you'll find in wine country or the coastside towns. Yet you can ride your bike from Cazadero to all the attractions of northern Sonoma County, then return to revel in the shady peace and quiet.

To reach Cazadero from Santa Rosa, drive north on 101 to River Road. Turn left toward Fulton and drive all the way to Guerneville. Turn right onto Highway 116 for about seven miles and take Cazadero Highway on the right another seven miles into town. From Highway 1 you can pick up 116 just south of Jenner to Cazadero Highway on the left.

On your bike, you have two options from 116 into Cazadero. For a fast, smooth, slightly downhill ride, take Cazadero Highway on the west side of the bridge over Austin Creek. For the scenic, hilly route, make your turn onto Austin Creek Road on the east side of the bridge. The two roads intersect about halfway to town; from there on, Austin Creek Road dishes out some steep climbs with sharp turns. You can easily avoid them by turning right onto Cazadero Highway at the intersection.

Establishments that rented cottages in 1988 include: Cazanoma Lodge (707-632-5255), up Kid Creek Road, features a German/American restaurant for your breakfasts and dinners; Elim Grove (707-632-5259), right on Cazadero Highway, serves more traditional fare. If your budget tells you

you'd rather camp, call the Russian River District of the State Parks Department (707-865-2391) for information on campgrounds in the area.

Karl Kneip, who often hosts groups from Western Wheelers Bicycle Club at his Cazadero cabin, put these two circuit, or loop, rides together. The routes are long and challenging, with plenty of nontrivial climbing. The hills in this part of the coast ranges are steep and the country roads are narrow. So when you find yourself pumping up Fort Ross Road or Joy Road, don't say I didn't warn you!

Circuit #1: Fort Ross

You can start this 40-mile loop to Fort Ross State Historical Park and back right in "downtown" Cazadero (which is, in effect, the General Store). About half a mile north of the General Store, across yet another bridge over Austin Creek, Cazadero Highway bears left and becomes Fort Ross Road. And on Fort Ross Road you'll immediately start your first stiff ascent, some 1300 feet of climbing in three miles.

The worst will be over in less than a mile, but you'll still need to crest Blue Jay Ridge. Then it's on to Brain Ridge and Creighton Ridge. At the last summit, you'll see the remains of the Creighton Ridge forest fire, which came right up to the road and the lovely homestead on the other side before it was contained.

Now you'll roll along to the intersection with Meyers Grade, where Fort Ross Road kind of doglegs to the right. In half a mile Fort Ross Road makes a sharp left turn down to Highway 1. Climbing it in the other direction, this 2.6-mile drop is one of the infamous groaners on the Terrible Two double century. We didn't take it, mostly because the redwood trees tend to make some of the steepest slopes "slippery as whale snot."

To ensure staying upright on your way down to the water, follow our lead: Turn right onto Seaview Road and ride the four miles of open country to Timber Cove Road. The bottom actually comes out about a mile south of Timber Cove, home of a rather interesting piece of statuary by Bufano. If you want to inspect it, you'll need to turn north into the wind back up to Timber Cove.

To reach Fort Ross, turn left on Highway 1 and then right at the park entrance. If you've never visited this memorial to Russo-California history, it's well worth the stop. You can ride a short paved path from the Visitor's Center down to the restored fort, pick up a personal cassette player for a few rubles, and take a walking tour in about a half hour. The restrooms are a rider's delight. And there's a small store where you can purchase some calorie replacement.

Back out on Highway 1, you have 12.5 miles of absolutely gorgeous scenery to cover on the way to Jenner. I am not exaggerating. Of all the vistas I've pedaled by, stopped at and photographed, the views on this section of the Coast Highway are the only ones that continue to blow me away every time I come upon them.

Finally, you'll twist and turn down one last plunge to beach level and enter the coastside tourist trap of Jenner. There's plenty of food and amenities here, but we opted to hang on for four more miles to Duncans Mills. Just south of Jenner, make a left onto Highway 116 and follow the river. You'll recognize the small-gauge railway display and Duncans Mills Deli & Restaurant right away. (The pasta at the Deli is first-rate!) It's just another mile and a half to the turn-off for Cazadero Highway and/or Austin Creek, whichever route you choose to return to your digs in Cazadero.

Circuit #2: Occidental via Bodega

This 50-miler starts and ends easy, but it has a few surprises along the way! Ride up to Highway 116 on Cazadero Highway. Turn left and get the into-the-wind ride to Jenner done before the afternoon breezes come up.

At Highway 1, turn south (left) for an eight-mile tailwind zip down to Bodega Bay. Just before you reach the main part of town, look for Bay Hill Road on the left. Studying the map last year, we thought Bay Hill was going to be a killer, but it turned out to be a relatively easy four-mile rolling climb.

You'll come out at Highway 1 where it cuts off from the coast toward Valley Ford. Turn left for a quick mile, then left again on Bodega Highway. You may want to stop in Bodega to check out the General Store and assorted curio shops, or just to refill your water bottle and make a pit stop.

Continuing on Bodega Highway, you'll come to Joy Road on the left in about another mile. Take it from me, there is no joy on Joy Road — at

least not in this direction! It is four miles of bitter uphill climbing that gets steeper with every turn of the cranks. About the third or fourth time that you're convinced you are really going to die right here and now, the pavement flattens out at the

Bodega Bay is a great place to stop for lunch along the Sonoma coast. corner of Bittner

13

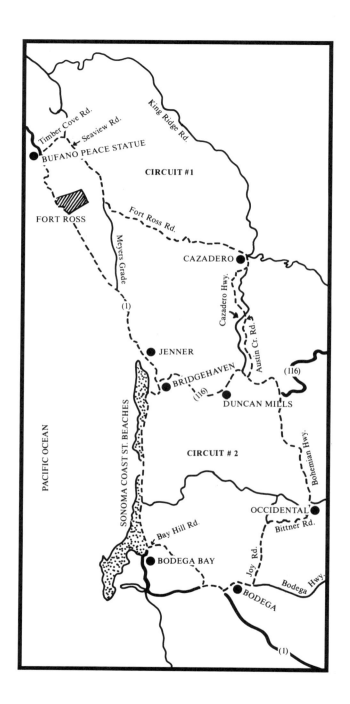

Timber Cove Rd.

King Ridge Rd.

Seaview Rd.

BUFANO PEACE STATUE

CIRCUIT #1

Fort Ross Rd.

FORT ROSS

Meyers Grade

CAZADERO

(1)

Cazadero Hwy.

Austin Cr. Rd.

JENNER

(116)

BRIDGEHAVEN

(116)

DUNCAN MILLS

PACIFIC OCEAN

SONOMA COAST ST. BEACHES

CIRCUIT # 2

Bohemian Hwy.

OCCIDENTAL

Bay Hill Rd.

Bittner Rd.

BODEGA BAY

Joy Rd.

Bodega Hwy.

BODEGA

(1)

14

Road. Take it to the right and you'll plunge into Occidental, where you can refuel on the most filling Italian food in existence. All-time Western Wheelers favorite: The Union Hotel just off Bohemian Highway; you can't miss it. Or try Negri's just around the corner.

With your tummy full and your lungs and legs working again, you'll be ready to pedal the mostly downhill seven miles on Bohemian Highway, back to 116. You'll pass right by Monte Rio, which Karl recommends only for water, "unless you've never been to the Pink Elephant." Don't ask me, I've never been there! I get the impression it's a bar/pool hall with plenty of local color.

At 116, turn left back toward the coast and you'll be at Austin Creek in about three more miles. This is a good time to take the "scenic route" on Austin Creek Road, a fitting finish to your final Cazadero circuit. Once you're back in town, you may just have time to take a well-deserved dip in the creek, relax with a drink and pore over the maps to plan circuit rides for your next visit.

P.S. If you're looking for an easy out-and-back with a scenic reward for those less inclined to suffer on steep hills, send 'em eight miles up 116 from Cazadero to Guerneville and 2.3 miles up Armstrong Redwoods Road to Armstrong Redwoods State Park. Be sure they take a camera!

ROUTE SLIPS

Circuit #1: Fort Ross
From Cazadero General Store

TURN	ON	FOR
Left	Cazadero Highway	0.4
Bear Left	Fort Ross Road	3.0
	1300-foot climb!	
Bear Right	Fort Ross Road	0.5
	At Meyers Grade	
Right	Seaview Road	4.0
Left	Timber Cove Road	3.0
Left	Highway 1	3.5
	Fort Ross State Historical Park on right	
Continue	Highway 1	12.5
Left	Highway 116	5.5
Left	Cazadero Highway	7.0

Circuit #2: Occidental
From Cazadero General Store

Right	Cazadero Highway	7.0
Right	Highway 116	5.5

Left	Highway 1	8.0
Left	Bay Hill Road	4.0
Left	Highway 1	1.0
Left	Bodega Highway	1.5
	Store, restrooms and water in Bodega	
Left	Joy Road	5.0
	Gear way down!	
Right	Bittner Road	2.0
	Pasta galore in Occidental!	
Left	Bohemian Highway	9.0
Left	Highway 116	3.0
Right	Austin Creek Road	4.0
Right	Cazadero Highway	1.5

Wine Country Rides without the Crowds
July 1987

Quick — name the most typical Northern California bike tour. Five will get you ten you said, "wine country." Another five says what you were really thinking was, "Napa Valley."

Folks come from everywhere to pedal from winery to winery in Napa. Too bad so many of them miss out on the wine country next door in Sonoma County. It's got something Napa lost a long time ago — peace and quiet.

The roads leading to the many excellent wineries in Sonoma County are practically empty compared to the traffic jams on Napa Valley's Highway 29, Silverado Trail and the cross roads between the two. Even Highway 128 through wine-rich Alexander Valley can be almost traffic free in the cool (and therefore prime riding time) of the morning.

To explore these quiet country roads, choose a flat-to-rolling loop to Geyserville and back, or a more challenging hilly one out to Monte Rio. These rides are similar to a couple Al Forkosh put together years ago, both of which I've covered in the past. This time, however, I've based them on the Santa Rosa Cycling Club's early-May century called — naturally — the Wine Country Century.

Both tours start in Fulton, north of Santa Rosa and about half a mile east of Highway 101 at the intersection of Fulton and River roads. There's a small market, but if you're in need of gas, water or bathrooms, best make a stop farther south at the intersection of Fulton and Guerneville roads, the last outpost of shopping-mall civilization.

Circling the Russian River

This 55-mile loop, the first half of the Wine Country Century, circles the Russian River, bypassing Healdsburg, doubling back from Geyserville and returning down Alexander Valley. Except for a three-mile climb up Chalk Hill Road, it's almost all flat or rolling hills. Along the way you'll view endless vineyards and have more than a few chances to stop and taste some top-notch vintages.

There's plenty of flat ranchland to warm up with as you ride west on River Road, then turn right on Laughlin. At the Y, bear left and skirt the south end of the County Airport. At Slusser Road, make another right, ride about 0.75 mile, and turn left on Station Road.

In about 2.75 miles you'll arrive at Eastside Road. Turn right, then jog left to stay on Eastside as it makes a circle back towards Wohler Road and the Russian River. Turn right on Wohler and follow it over the old steel bridge, which deserves a snapshot or two if you've brought your camera.

On the other side, you'll circle around a bit more to Westside Road, where the rolling hills — and the vineyards — begin in earnest. Don't miss Hop Kiln Winery on your right. Look for the National Historic Landmark sign and the huge wine barrels at the entrance.

In a little less than nine miles, you'll come to West Dry Creek Road. A right turn here will take you via Westside into Healdsburg, where you can find food, water and relief if you need them. Otherwise, turn left to tackle more rolling hills along West Dry Creek Road. The vineyards of the Russian River valley are spread out on your right as you parallel Dry Creek for another nine miles.

Take care not to pass Yoakim Bridge Road, where a right turn will bring you out to Dry Creek Road. Turn right here and then make the very next left onto Canyon Road. In two miles cross Highway 101 and turn right on Highway 128 to ride into Geyserville. Since this is your turn-around point (it's a little more than halfway on the loop), it's the ideal place to stop for lunch. Some of the best wine tasting is coming up, and you'll want a full stomach for the venture.

After lunch, follow Highway 128 as it turns right and enters Alexander Valley. If the tourists are out in full force, here's where you'll find them. You'll also find some truly great wineries, including the Alexander Valley Winery on your left (it's my favorite for whites).

You'll leave the tourists behind when you turn left onto Red Winery Road for a four-mile break. As you make a broad right turn to stay on Red Winery Road, look back over your shoulder at the elegant white mansion that looks like part of the "Falcon Crest" set.

At Pine Flat Road, make a right and ride down to Jimtown (there's a store here), where you'll make a left onto 128 again. In about three miles, turn right on Chalk Hill Road and prepare to climb. The going gets pretty

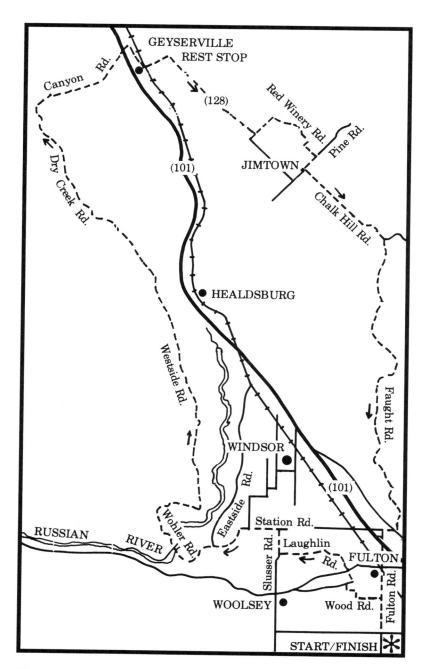

GEYSERVILLE
REST STOP

Canyon Rd.

(128)

Red Winery Rd.

Pine Rd.

Dry Creek Rd.

(101)

JIMTOWN

Chalk Hill Rd.

● HEALDSBURG

Westside Rd.

Faught Rd.

WINDSOR

Eastside Rd.

(101)

Station Rd.

Wohler Rd.

Laughlin

RUSSIAN

RIVER

Slusser Rd.

Rd.

FULTON

Fulton Rd.

WOOLSEY ●

Wood Rd.

START/FINISH ✳

steep for about five miles, but then you'll fly downhill to Faught Road. Make a left and follow Faught for about a mile and a quarter to Old Redwood Highway. At Airport Boulevard turn left, then left again onto Fulton Road to return to your start.

Up to Monte Rio

There are fewer wineries, and more hills, on the second half of the Wine Country Century, a 50-mile ride over the ridge to the west. From Fulton, ride south on Fulton Road and turn right on Piner Road. In 2.5 miles, turn left on Olivet, ride for about a mile and turn right on Guerneville Road. At Frei Road, make a left and start the long climb up toward Occidental.

Keep pumping and before you know it you'll be plummeting downhill. Don't miss the right turn on Bohemian Highway at the bottom. (Turn left if you want to go into town.) You'll ride another five miles of mostly downhill to reach Monte Rio, where you can also get the usual amenities towns offer.

After you cross the Monte Rio bridge, turn right on Highway 116 and follow the signs to Guerneville. You'll make another right on 116 at the stop sign, in order to cross another bridge. Keep a sharp lookout for the next turn at the fork, where 116 turns left and Neeley takes off on the right. In between the two, you'll turn right onto Mays Canyon Road.

It's three miles until you pick up 116 again, and before you do, you'll get some aerobic exercise! The climb grows steadily, culminating in a 13 + % grade at the top!

Turn right onto 116 and take it easy for a mile or so. You'll make another right onto Green Valley Road, which bears left in about two miles. Then it's another uphill grunt (the steepest of the ride). Okay, you can relax; the worst is over. At Vine Hill Road, turn left and coast down to Laguna Road, where another left will bring you out to River Road.

Turn right and in about a mile, look for Woolsey Road veering off on your right. You'll think the climbing has started again, but it's just a short pitch to bring you up above and paralleling River Road for about two miles. At Wood Road, turn right, then left onto Fulton Road, and back to your start.

ROUTE SLIPS
Circling Russian River
From Fulton and River Roads north of Santa Rosa

TURN	ON	FOR
West	River Road	1.0
Right	Laughlin	2.25
Bear Left	At Y	
	Around County Airport	
Right	Slusser Road	0.75

Left	Station Road	2.5
Right/Left	Eastside Road	0.1
Right	Wohler Road	2.3
	Over bridge	
Right	Westside Road	8.8
Left	West Dry Creek Road	9.0
	Food, water, restrooms in Healdsburg, to the right	
Right	Yoakim Bridge Road	1.0
Right	Dry Creek Road	0.5
Left	Canyon Road	2.0
Right	Highway 128	1.0
	Food in Geyserville	
Right	Highway 128	4.0
Left	Red Winery Road	3.3
Right	Pine Flat Road	0.25
Left	Highway 128	4.25
Right	Chalk Hill Road	11.5
	Gear down!	
Left	Faught Road	1.5
Right	Airport Boulevard	0.25
Left	Fulton Road	
	To River Road	

Up to Monte Rio

From Fulton and River Roads north of Santa Rosa

TURN	ON	FOR
South	Fulton Road	2.5
Right	Piner Road	3.0
Left	Olivet	1.0
Right	Guerneville Road	2.0
Left	Frei Road	1.5
Continue	Graton Road	6.0
	At Highway 116	
Right	Bohemian Highway	8.0
Right	Highway 116	4.5
	After Monte Rio bridge	
	Follow signs to Guerneville	
Right	Highway 116	0.75
	Across bridge	
Right	Mays Canyon Road	3.0
	Where 116 turns left at Neely	
	Gear down!	
Right	116	1.0

Right	Green Valley Road	8.0
	Time to gear down again!	
Left	Vine Hill Road	2.75
Left	Laguna Road	0.2
Right	River Road	1.0
Right	Woolsey Road	2.0
Right	Wood Road	3.25
Left	Fulton Road	0.8
	To River Road	

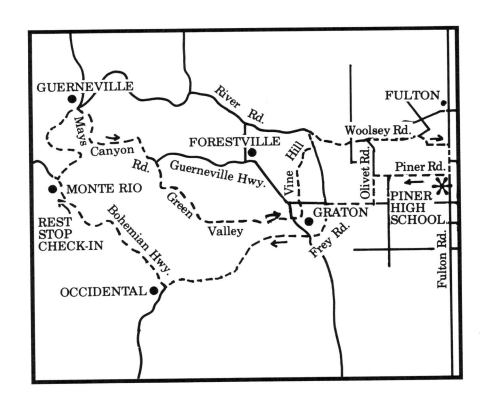

Napa-Sonoma History Tour
November 1990

For your history lesson this month, boys and girls, we're going to take a bike ride to Sonoma. This little town in the heart of California wine country is the cradle of our state's independence from Mexico, and the northernmost outpost of the Spanish padres' Mission Trail. Starting from Napa, we'll cover 42 miles of rolling hills (no major climbs), with another historical stop along the way on the Napa River.

Our starting place is the Bicycle Works, at Redwood Plaza on Solano Avenue in Napa. You can tell what kind of shop the owners, Bob and Mary Hillhouse, are running by the sign on the door — "Shirtless, Shoeless, Food, Drink & Children Welcome Here." When you drop in for that replacement patch kit or forgotten pump, ask if they have any copies left of *Bicycle Rides in and around Napa Valley,* prepared by the (now defunct) Napa Bicycle Club.

This ride is a combination of two in the club's booklet, compiled by one Austin Miller, who also serves up local points of interest, campgrounds and wineries. (You'll find another excellent source of cyclist-oriented Sonoma history on pages 5 through 17 of *A Bicyclist's Guide to Bay Area History* by Carol O'Hare, available at almost any Bay Area bike shop.)

Although Miller did his level best to provide detours on quiet, vineyard-lined back roads, be warned that any pedal touring in the Napa/Sonoma wine country involves riding on the narrow shoulders of State Highway 121 alongside heavy motor traffic. The vineyards, by the way, are a special visual treat this time of year, when the vines are coming off their peak of brilliant fall colors.

First stop is Cuttings Wharf, a couple miles off 121 just south of Napa. According to Miller, "Out there at Cuttings Wharf are...ghosts...[from when]...silent sailing vessels picked up and deposited passengers and cargo here as far back as the 1850s." Now all that's left are a few pilings, a fishing pier, and a newly erected plaque that fills you in on the significance of the site.

Then it's back out to the vineyards and orchards for a rolling ride that circles south of Sonoma, then approaches the Town Plaza and Park from the west. Most of the old adobes, as well as the Mission San Francisco Solano de Sonoma, are on Spain Street on the opposite end of the Plaza from your entry on Napa Street.

Founded in 1823, the Mission was apparently more of an attempt to halt the advance of the Russians already settled in at Fort Ross and Bodega than to bring Christianity to the Indians. It marks the northern end of "El Camino Real," the road connecting all 21 missions throughout Spanish Colonial America, from Guatemala on up.

General Vallejo arrived in Sonoma in 1834 and proceeded to build the place into a bastion of Mexican military defense. Much good it did him. Upset with restrictions on land acquisition, the growing gringo population revolted in 1846. On June 14, they captured Sonoma, took General Vallejo prisoner, and declared a free and independent Republic of California, raising a homemade "Bear Flag" in the Plaza.

In less than a month California was annexed by the United States, war with Mexico was imminent, and the Bear Flag became the official state flag. Check out the monument commemorating the whole twist of history, across Spain Street from the Sonoma Barracks, our first "state capitol."

Other historical "musts" on Miller's list include the Swiss Hotel on Spain Street and the Depot Museum on First Street West. You can join a walking tour at the Chamber of Commerce in the old Public Library building at the edge of the park, where you'll also find water and public restrooms.

By now you're probably hungry and thirsty. There's plenty to eat and drink, from sandwiches to lemonade to ice cream bars and frozen yogurt, at the Sonoma Cheese Factory, right in the middle of Spain Street. For a sit-down meal, there's no shortage of fine restaurants all around you.

Well fortified, we'll set out on our return to Napa via the smooth pavement and wide shoulder on Napa Road. If the winds are prevailing, they'll be behind us, so we'll scoot out to Highway 121, where a tough uphill left turn into the heavy traffic will jolt us back to reality. Then we'll retrace our tire tracks (skipping the side trip to Cuttings Wharf) back to downtown Napa.

ROUTE SLIP

From Redwood Plaza, Solano & Redwood Streets in Napa

TURN	ON	FOR
Right	Solano Avenue	1.0
Left	F Street	0.1
Right	Coffield	0.1
Continue	Bike path	0.4
Left	First Street	0.1
Continue	Freeway Drive	1.3
Continue	Golden Gate Drive	1.8
Left	Stanley Lane	0.1
Right	Highway 12/121	1.3
Left	Cuttings Wharf Road	2.5
Reverse	Cuttings Wharf Road	1.0
Left	Las Amigas Road	2.0
Left	Duhig Road	0.6
	Becomes Ramal Road	
Right	Ramal Road	6.6
Left	Highway 12/121	1.3
	Caution! Heavy traffic and no shoulder!	
Right	Broadway/Highway 12	1.9
Left	Watmaugh Road	1.3
Right	Arnold Drive	2.3
Right	Petaluma Avenue	0.6
Right	Riverside Drive	0.1
Continue	West Napa Street	0.1
	Sonoma Town Plaza on left.	
Left	First Street	0.1
Right	Spain Street	0.1
Right	Third Street	0.1
Left	East Napa Street	1.0
Right	Eighth Street	1.2
Left	Napa Road	3.1
Left	Highway 12/121	4.9
Left	Stanley Lane	0.1
	No sign except "Begin Freeway"!	
Right	Golden Gate Drive	1.8
Continue	Freeway Drive	1.3
Left	Bike Path	0.4
	Sharp left after light	
Continue	Coffield	0.1
Right	F Street	0.1
Left	Solano Avenue	1.0
Left	Redwood Plaza	

Long-Distance Training Rides in Marin
April 1990

As I write this column, winter still reigns. It's bitter cold one day, foggy or rainy the next. Who wants to get out and ride long distances now?

But winter has this annual habit of turning into spring. And with spring come centuries. If you haven't trained all winter, you're just not ready to tackle 100 miles featuring thousands of feet of climbing.

That was the problem facing Western Wheeler Leo Moll a few years ago. Leo wanted to do a string of centuries, culminating in the Davis Double in May. But he just wasn't motivated to train over long, hilly miles in the dead of winter. As much as actual training, Leo figured he needed support. So he put together a series of rides starting in January and running through May for what he called a Long Distance Training and Support Group (LDTSG) of club riders who wanted to be ready when spring — and centuries — sprung.

The rides featured at least four separate routes, each designed for a different training level. So LDTSG worked for almost everyone in the club from experienced, strong racer types who were used to training year-round to newer, slower riders who wanted to get faster or train for their first century. All the routes converged at the same lunch spot, where everyone could sit in on a short "seminar" on some aspect of training such as stretching, nutrition or gearing.

The response was tremendous. Over 100 club members came out for some rides. Even bitter cold mornings or the threat of rain didn't deter many of them from riding over the mountains to the coast or across the bay to the East Bay Hills.

Soon Leo realized he needed even more support, and not just for training. LDTSG was turning into a full time job! He appealed to his training buddies for help in planning routes, drawing maps, leading rides and conducting seminars. Today LDTSG is run by committee. Volunteers lead the seminars, and a different leader (or team of leaders) takes full responsibility for the LDTSG ride each week.

The turnouts have grown to over 150 riders, even for some rides that require carpooling from Western Wheelers territory on the Peninsula to faraway places like Monterey or Marin.

To understand a multi-route LDTSG ride map, you need a quick rundown of Western Wheelers rider classifications: B denotes a "cruising pace" on the flat of 10 to 12 miles per hour. C denotes 13 to 15 mph, D is 16 to 18 mph, and E, 19 to off the speedometer scale. (Climbing paces are obviously much slower, descending faster.) The higher the classification, the more mileage and elevation gain can be expected on the corresponding LDTSG route.

Typically, Ds and Es start at a later time or from a point further away from the lunch spot than the Bs and Cs. The cleverest ride leaders (or at least those lucky enough to draw a location with lots of different ways to get from point A to point B) arrange for everyone to gather at the same time and starting point.

John Walker pulled it off for 1990s LDTSG in Marin County, which took place the last weekend in February. Everyone started at 8:30 a.m. from the Marinwood Community Center on Miller Creek Road, next to the fire station just off Lucas Valley Road. The Bs did about 53 miles and 2,300 feet of climbing. The Cs had 80 miles to cover, with 3,500 feet. Ds did a similar route to the Cs, except they got to go out to the coast and climb the Marshall Wall, for 97.5 miles and over 4500 feet.

Only the three Es brave enough to do the whole route were faced with both the Marshall Wall and the 10% climb (with 14% pitch!) on Balboa Road, for 109 miles and over 6,000 grueling uphill feet. True to form, each route featured a lunch stop at the Marin Cheese Factory on Red Hill Road (also called Point Reyes-Petaluma Road), where many sampled the primo Brie and Camembert.

The B riders got to warm up fast. The only group to ride west on Lucas Valley Road, they faced a 7% climb within the first ten miles, then crossed a ridge on Nicasio Valley Road in the next four. Although they got to relax

The Cheese Factory is the perfect spot for a lunch break for each of these training rides.

on Sir Francis Drake Boulevard for a while, they faced the climb through Samuel P. Taylor State Park to reach the coast. Then they got to check out easy-going Bear Valley Road on the edge of Point Reyes National Seashore before turning back toward the Cheese Factory. Their return after lunch was a short (but often bumpy) 16-mile jaunt back to Marinwood through Novato.

Meanwhile, the Cs, Ds, and Es started on the Marinwood Bike Path paralleling Highway 101, and headed over the rough, pot-hole ridden streets of Novato to Point Reyes-Petaluma Road. In Petaluma, the Cs cut out along Hicks Valley Road (formerly Wilson Hill Road), and the Ds and Es headed up Spring Hill Road to Tomales.

While the Cs explored the easy rollers on Chileno Valley Road on their way to Petaluma, the Ds and Es made separate tracks for the coast, where the Es tackled Balboa and descended Limantour Road to rejoin the Ds at Bear Valley. Then both turned back inland to meet the Cs on the way back to the Cheese Factory.

After lunch, Cs, Ds and Es picked up the same route back toward the coast, but the Cs cut over to Sir Francis Drake on Platform Bridge Road, while the Ds and Es looped back on Highway 1. Then all headed back to Marinwood via Nicasio Valley and the shady side of Lucas Valley Road.

Truth to tell, there's a lot of route swapping and improvisation on LDTSG rides. Bs often choose to do the C route at a slower pace, Cs the D route, and so on. On the other hand, Es who might be feeling a little under the weather will switch to the D or C route, and so on down. Some have also been known to combine two routes where they see the opportunity. It seems as if the unofficial club motto is, "If you don't like the route, go out and make up one of your own!"

Need I point out that you can do the same? Maybe you'd like to start out on the C, but find you're still feeling strong when you get to Petaluma. Try heading out on the D to do the Wall. Of, if you find you've bitten off more than you can chew on the E route, switch to the D and skip the Balboa climb. It's all the same, as long as you get a good long-distance workout to build on the following week.

If you've never ridden in northern Marin and southern Sonoma counties before, be prepared for no shoulders on many rural roads, heavy traffic on Sir Francis Drake east of Highway 1, and the bucolic aroma of dairy cattle and their habitat. You'll also discover light traffic on nearly every back road, charming scenery and coastal breezes. Enjoy!

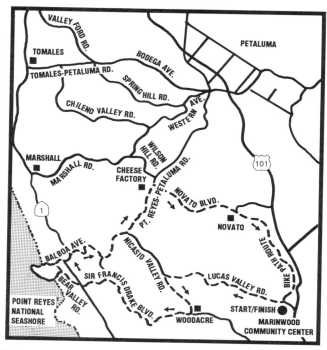

ROUTE SLIPS

All rides start from the Marinwood Community Center on Miller Creek Road off Lucas Valley Road.

B Ride: Cheese Factory Loop

TURN	ON	FOR
Left	Miller Creek Road	0.1
Right	Lucas Valley	9.3
Left	Nicasio Valley	3.7
Right	Sir Francis Drake	9.7
Right	Highway 1	0.1
Left	Bear Valley Road	2.3
	Check out the Point Reyes Visitors Center	
Right	Sir Francis Drake	1.0
Left	Highway 1	0.7
	Through Point Reyes Station	
Right	Point Reyes-Petaluma	9.5
Left	Cheese Factory	
Left	Point Reyes-Petaluma	0.5
	AKA Red Hill Road to Petaluma, then becomes D Street	

Right	Novato Boulevard	9.8
	Downhill, then potholes	
Right	Sunset Parkway	1.0
Left	Ignacio Boulevard	1.7
Right	Alameda Del Prado	1.5
Straight	Bike Path	1.0
	Exit at intersection of Miller Creek and Marinwood Avenue	
Straight	Miller Creek	1.1
Right	Marinwood Community Center	

C Ride: Chileno Valley Romp

TURN	ON	FOR
Left	Miller Creek	1.1
Left	Bike Path	1.0
	On left side of road at Marinwood Avenue	
Right	Alameda Del Prado	1.5
Left	Ignacio Boulevard	1.7
Right	Sunset Parkway	1.0
Left	Novato Boulevard	9.8
Right	Point Reyes-Petaluma	0.5

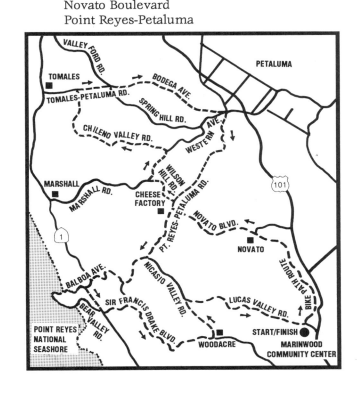

Left	Wilson Hill/Hicks Valley Road	2.7
	Sign reads: Hicks Valley Road	
Right	Marshall-Petaluma	2.5
Left	Chileno Valley	9.8
Right	Tomales Road	1.9
Continue	Bodega Avenue	7.6
Right	Webster	0.3
Left	Western Avenue	0.2
Right	Fair Street	0.5
Continue	Tenth Street	0.1
Right	D Street	4.0
Continue	Point Reyes-Petaluma	4.2
Right	Cheese Factory	
	Lunch stop	
Right	Point Reyes-Petaluma	6.4
Left	Platform Bridge Road	2.4
Left	Sir Francis Drake	7.9
	Heavy traffic, no shoulder!	
Left	Nicasio Valley	3.7
	One more ridge to cross!	
Right	Lucas Valley	9.3
Left	Miller Creek	0.1
Right	Marinwood Community Center	

D Ride: Here Today, Gone Tomales

TURN	ON	FOR
Left	Miller Creek	1.1
Left	Bike Path	1.0
	On left side of road at Marinwood Avenue	
Right	Alameda Del Prado	1.5
Left	Ignacio Boulevard	1.7
Right	Sunset Parkway	4.3
Left	Novato Boulevard	9.8
Right	Point Reyes-Petaluma	7.9
	Becomes D Street	
Left	10th Street	0.1
Continue	Fair Street	0.5
Left	Western Avenue	1.3
Continue	Spring Hill	7.2
Left	Bodega Avenue	0.1
Left	Tomales Road	1.9
Continue	Tomales-Petaluma	5.2
Left	Highway 1	6.8

Left	Marshall-Petaluma	10.8
	Up the Wall!	
Right	Wilson Hill/Hicks Valley	2.7
Right	Point Reyes-Petaluma	0.9
Right	Cheese Factory	
	Lunch stop	
Right	Point Reyes-Petaluma	9.5
Left	Highway 1	0.8
Right	Sir Francis Drake	0.7
Left	Bear Valley	2.3
	Check out the Visitor Center	
Right	Highway 1	0.1
Left	Sir Francis Drake	9.7
	Heavy traffic!	
Left	Nicasio Valley	3.7
	One more ridge to cross!	
Right	Lucas Valley	9.3
Left	Miller Creek	0.1
Right	Marinwood Community Center	

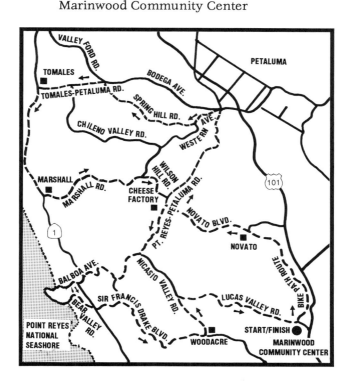

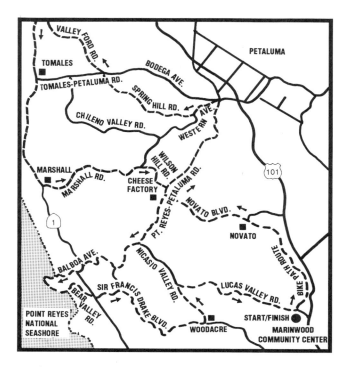

E Ride: Noriega's Revenge
(The first white man to cross Panama was Balboa.)

TURN	ON	FOR
Left	Miller Creek	1.1
Left	Bike Path	1.0
	On left side of road at Marinwood Avenue	
Right	Alameda Del Prado	1.5
Left	Ignacio Boulevard	1.7
Right	Sunset Parkway	1.0
Left	Novato Boulevard	9.8
Right	Point Reyes-Petaluma	7.9
	Becomes D Street	
Left	10th Street	0.1
Continue	Fair Street	0.5
Left	Western Avenue	1.3
	Start climbing again!	
Continue	Spring Hill	7.2
	No major climbs here, just dairy cows!	
Left	Bodega Avenue	0.1

Straight	Petaluma-Valley Ford	8.1
Left	Highway 1	12.1
	Sign missing! Look for direction sign for	
	Valley Ford and Tomales	
Left	Marshall-Petaluma	10.8
	Up the Wall!	
Right	Wilson Hill/Hicks Valley	2.7
Right	Point Reyes-Petaluma	0.9
Right	Cheese Factory	
Right	Point Reyes-Petaluma	9.5
Left	Highway 1	0.8
Right	Sir Francis Drake	0.9
Left	Balboa	1.5
	Details: 800 feet up; 10% grade (one 14% pitch)!	
	Ignore "Not a Through Street" sign, ride through	
	fence at top.	
Left	Limantour	3.7
Left	Bear Valley	1.8
Right	Highway 1	0.1
Left	Sir Francis Drake	9.7
	Heavy traffic!	
Left	Nicasio Valley	3.7
	One more ridge to cross!	
Right	Lucas Valley	9.3
Left	Miller Creek	0.1
Right	Marinwood Community Center	

Killer Hills North:
Upward Bound in Marin and Napa
April 1986

At long last, we look north of San Francisco Bay for hills that can qualify as killers. There is a logical reason why I've been holding this region back. While I'd been deviously saving Napa County's Oakville Grade for this series, I despaired of ever finding a true killer hill in Marin County.

You see, a hill that's really a killer is one that represents more threat than challenge. Every time the possibility of climbing it arises, a route around it suddenly sounds much better. Although many who've ridden them talk about Marin's Marshall Wall or Mt. Tam as though they were killers, neither seemed especially threatening to me. A true killer hill, I reasoned, ought to include at least one pitch that is both extra long and extra steep, and neither filled that requirement.

Grant Petersen came to my rescue with a little hill described in *Roads To Ride*. It may be only a couple miles long, but it's a steady, straight climb all the way, with not a switchback in sight. Besides, the rest of the route is quite scenic, providing incentive to keep going. After all, the only way to deal effectively with a killer hill is to get out and ride it. A few successes, and it will turn into a climb you can brag about instead of avoid.

Oakville Grade

Until 1985, Oakville Grade was the *pièce de résistance* on the Tour of the Napa Valley Century. Increasing numbers of riders, heavy traffic and pressure from the authorities resulted in its removal from the century route, but that doesn't mean you can't ride it on your own.

For a good, long warm-up, start in Napa at the corner of Trancas Street and the Silverado Trail. You'll get to ride north on Silverado, past vineyards and wineries, for nearly eleven miles before you have to make a turn.

When you do, it will be a left onto Oakville Cross Road, where you can find plenty of pit stops and way stations. Then make a left on Highway 128, using extra caution to deal with wine-tasting motorists.

Oakville Grade will be on your right in a mere quarter of a mile. Make the turn and gear down. It's about two miles of climbing, mostly in the open, with at least one mile of 16% to 19% grades! If you're tempted to tack to the top, keep in mind that drivers cresting the hill in the other direction

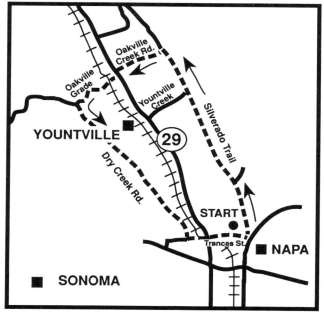

can't see you until the last minute. Remember, weekends bring out the heaviest, fastest-moving traffic.

Once over the worst part, you'll plunge to Dry Creek Road, where a left turn gives you over nine miles of gradual descent back to Napa. Make a left at Redwood Road, and cross Highway 29 to continue on Trancas to Silverado and the end of a 30-mile workout.

Balboa Discovery

The history books tell us that Señor Balboa discovered the Pacific Ocean. The killer hill on this 23-mile ride is Balboa Avenue, an appropriate name since it connects Inverness Park with Limantour Road, the back way into Point Reyes National Seashore. Limantour is also the direct way to the AYH Hostel there, giving overnight touring cyclists an alternate route to or from Samuel P. Taylor Park in Olema.

Start at Taylor Park headquarters on Sir Francis Drake Boulevard and ride 1.75 miles to Platform Bridge Road. Turn right for 2.25 miles of pancake-flat road and beautiful scenery. At Point Reyes-Petaluma Road, turn left and continue to Highway 1, turn left for half a mile, then right back onto Sir Francis Drake.

After the gradual 1.25-mile upgrade to Inverness Park, turn left on Balboa Avenue at its junction with Portola Avenue. The climb is narrow, straight as an arrow, with minimal traffic. There's a 14% grade right off the bat, which eases out to an average of 10% before you finish the first mile.

Limantour Road sits at the top of Balboa. If you're headed for the Youth Hostel, turn right and look for the AYH sign in about two miles. Otherwise, turn left for the four-mile downhill to Bear Valley Road. Take a right and ride out to Highway 1. You might want to make a stop at the Park Service's Bear Valley Visitors Center on the way.

At Highway 1, make a right turn, then a left in Olema onto Sir Francis Drake. It's about four miles back to Samuel P. Taylor Park headquarters, starting with a long, open climb. Once past Platform Bridge Road, you're back in the redwoods that make this ride so enjoyable.

ROUTE SLIPS

Oakville Grade

From Trancas Street and Silverado Trail in Napa

TURN	ON	FOR
North	Silverado Trail	10.7
Left	Oakville Cross Road	2.5
Left	Highway 128	0.25
Right	Oakville Grade	3.8
	Approximately 2.0 miles to summit	
Left	Dry Creek Road	9.3
Left	Redwood Road	1.0
Continue	Trancas Street	2.0
	To Silverado Trail	

Balboa

From Samuel P. Taylor Park Headquarters

TURN	ON	FOR
West	Sir Francis Drake Boulevard	1.75
Right	Platform Bridge Road	2.25
Left	Point Reyes-Petaluma Road	3.0
Left	Highway 1	0.50
Right	Sir Francis Drake	1.25
Left	Balboa Avenue	2.3
	At Portola Avenue	
Left	Limantour Road	4.0
Right	Bear Valley Road	2.5
Right	Highway 1	1.75
Left	Sir Francis Drake	4.0
	To Samuel P. Taylor Park Headquarters	

2. SAN FRANCISCO PENINSULA
San Francisco, San Mateo, Santa Clara Counties

Here's the premier riding region of the Bay Area. The Peninsula runs from San Francisco south to Silicon Valley and has more roads than you can shake a frame pump at. Explore the Santa Cruz Mountain foothills. Cruise the 50+ miles of Skyline Drive, or head off road on the trails of the Midpeninsula Regional Open Space District. Visit horse country in Woodside, chart the San Andreas Fault through Portola Valley, and wander the flats in and around Stanford University. All prime Pedal Tour country!

Peninsula to San Francisco: Summer Music Ride
June 1986

This is the 49th summer during which free Sunday afternoon concerts have been presented in Sigmund Stern Grove, off Sloat Boulevard and 19th Avenue in San Francisco. Munching a picnic lunch at Stern Grove while enjoying live performances of Beethoven, Mozart, Dixieland, and opera (to name but a few) has become a Bay Area tradition.

Several years ago two South Bay bike clubs — Almaden and Skyline — began their own Stern Grove tradition of bicycling to the concerts from the lower Peninsula. Those who wanted to get in a century's worth of riding started from as far south as Cupertino. (Of course, no one complained that their 90-mile plus round trip was broken in half by a satisfying meal and a couple hours of music.) The saner group, out for a round trip of only 60 miles or so, joined up with them in Woodside.

Most of the ride from Woodside is up Skyline Drive/Highway 35, a "roller coaster" of climbs and descents that merges with Interstate 280 for a few miles in San Mateo. Steve Teng developed and fine-tuned this route to include bike paths for those unwilling to ride the freeway. He also planned a deli stop to buy that picnic lunch, and managed to avoid at least some of the inevitable traffic plaguing the neighborhoods around Stern Grove on Sunday afternoons.

If you're driving to Woodside, park at Woodside School, the former site of Woodside Town Hall, about a quarter of a mile west of Roberts Store at the corner of Highway 84 and Canada Road. Ride out to Canada, turn left and follow it all the way to the junction with Highway 92 at the edge of Lower Crystal Springs Reservoir.

Turn left at the light, then right onto Skyline Drive/Highway 35 where it merges briefly with Highway 92. You'll climb up along the upper reservoir and then cross the dam on a bridge. The next climb will bring you to the southern entrance to Sawyer Camp Trail on the left.

Although it's often referred to as a bike path, Sawyer Camp Trail is also used by joggers, strollers, skateboarders, and just about anyone else. It can get quite crowded during the middle of the day, but if you've started out early enough, you should have few problems negotiating the six miles of trail up to the San Andreas Reservoir. There are several semi-permanent portapotties along the way. At the end, you'll cross another dam and climb back up to Skyline at Hillcrest (check the view of the Bay!).

Turn left and ride on Skyline for about two blocks, to Larkspur. Turn left again and cross under Highway 280, then turn right at the dead end onto another bike path. You'll probably meet runners and walkers here, too, but not as many as on Sawyer Camp Trail. In a little less than two miles, you'll come out on Skyline again. Turn left to keep heading toward the city.

Stay on Skyline, with its ups and downs, right through the freeway interchange where Highways 1 and 35 literally cross each other in their rush to (or from) the city. The traffic zips by at 55 + mph, but the visibility is excellent and there are plenty of lanes for maneuvering. Use your effective cycling skills, plus a pinch of chutzpah, to merge left and stay on Skyline Drive.

When you reach Daly City, the first order of business will be a magnificent descent featuring a sweeping view of San Francisco. Then it's time to think about lunch and a pit stop. If you make a right on John Daly Boulevard, then turn right into Westlake Shopping Center, you'll find a marvelous little Italian delicatessen next to the pizza parlor. Stern Grove is a little more than three miles from here.

From the shopping center, turn left onto the Skyline frontage road, then right at the traffic light onto Lake Merced Boulevard. Ride up Lake Merced, past the San Francisco State campus, and make a right on Middlefield. Then it's a right on Sloat, an immediate left on El Mirasol, and a right on Crestlake. The entrance to Stern Grove will be on your left in a few short blocks. It's a short, steep descent down to the parking area, then a quick pedal past cars and pedestrians to the amphitheatre.

Lock up your bikes, find a good place to sit, and enjoy yourself. For the next few hours you'll be listening, not pedaling. If it's a sunny day, be prepared to feel the heat. The grove is deep and sheltered from the legendary Pacific breezes. Sunscreen and a hat will both come in handy. For cold drinks, visit the concession stands on the opposite side of the grove from where you entered (where you'll find the bathrooms, too).

When the concert's over, brace yourself for the ensuing traffic. Ride back past the parking lot and jockey with the motorists for the uphill climb to the street (be sure to gear down in plenty of time!). Turn right on Crestlake and ride along Pine Lake Park to give the traffic a chance to thin.

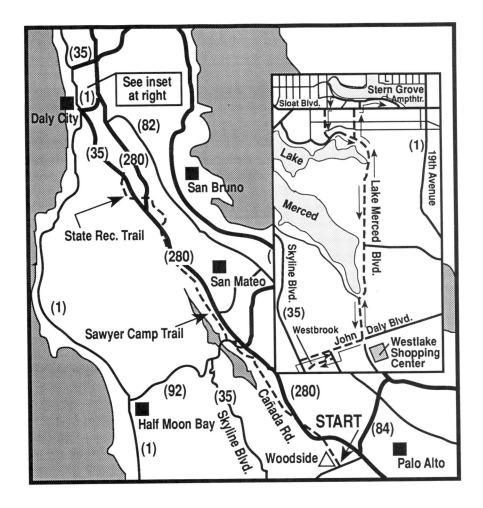

Turn left on Yorba, then left again on 34th Avenue. Cross Sloat, where 34th becomes Clearfield. Cross Ocean and turn left on Gellert, then right on Middlefield. Use caution making a left onto Lake Merced Boulevard. It's not a bad idea, once you've done so, to use the sidewalk/bike path on the right.

If you'd like to make another pit stop, turn left onto John Daly Boulevard and head back to Westlake Shopping Center. From the shopping center, turn left onto the frontage road, which becomes South Mayfair. Ride up the hill to Westridge, turn right and then left at the light onto Skyline. The rest of the way is a reverse of the route you followed in the morning. The sun will still be over your shoulder, and so will the wind in this direction.

If you'd like to bike to Stern Grove, allow enough riding and lunch-buying time to arrive by at least noon. The performance won't begin until 2:00, but the amphitheatre fills up hours earlier for the popular concerts. That kind of crowd makes it virtually impossible to keep your bike with you, so be sure to bring a lock.

One way to avoid the crunch is to reserve a picnic table by calling 415-398-6551 the previous Monday morning. Keep trying — there's only one line and it's usually busy. Reserved tables, by the way, are just as free as sitting on the benches or the lawn. Another possibility is to arrange with friends to bring blankets and a picnic hamper by car or bus and save you a seat.

ROUTE SLIP

From Woodside School on Highway 84 in Woodside

TURN	ON	FOR
Left	Woodside Road/Highway 84	0.25
Left	Canada Road	7.5
Left	Highway 92	0.75
Right	Skyline Drive/Highway 35	1.6
Left	Sawyer Camp Trail	6.0
Left	Skyline	0.6
Left	Larkspur	0.1
Right	CalTrans Recreational Trail	1.5
Left	Skyline Drive/Highway 35	8.0
	Merge left at freeway interchange to stay on 35	
Right	John Daly Boulevard	0.75
	Deli, restrooms at Westlake Shopping Center	
Left	Lake Merced Boulevard	2.5
Right	Middlefield	0.5
Right	Sloat	< 0.1
Immed. Left	El Mirasol	0.1
Right	Crestlake	0.25
Left	Stern Grove entrance	

Return:

Right	Crestlake	0.5
Left	Yorba	0.1
Left	24th Avenue	0.25
	Cross Sloat	
Continue	Clearfield	0.3

Left	Gellert	0.4
Right	Middlefield	< 0.1
Left	Lake Merced	2.5
Right	South Mayfair	
	Westlake Shopping Center on right	
Right	Westridge	< 0.1
Left	Skyline Drive/Highway 35	8.0
Right	CalTrans Recreational Trail	1.5
Left	Larkspur	0.1
Right	Skyline	0.6
Right	Sawyer Camp Trail	6.0
Right	Skyline Drive/Highway 35	1.6
Left	Highway 92	0.75
Right	Canada Road	7.5
Left	Woodside Road/Highway 84	0.25
Left	Woodside School	

Youth Hostel Stopovers: Overnight Tours Along the Coast
September 1984

Does the idea of staying in youth hostels conjure up images of touring the Swiss Alps or the flatlands of Holland? You don't have to pay an elaborate airfare to take advantage of the continental custom of hosteling. American Youth Hostels is turning hosteling into an American tradition. And the coast ranges of Northern California boast no less than seven hostels, some within easy biking distance of each other.

September is an ideal month to get away to a hostel. The tourists have gone home from their summer vacations. The weather is perfect for cycling. And you've had all summer to get in shape for carrying a load over the hills.

Not that you'll need to carry much. Hostels provide bedding, including a "sleep sack" made of sheets which you can rent for 50 cents a night. You can eat out at a local restaurant, or buy your food at a nearby grocery store and cook it in the hostel's well-equipped kitchen. That leaves you with only your tools, clothes, camera and other personal gear to fill your panniers.

Much of the information about the four hostels featured here came from a brochure available from the Golden Gate Council of AYH. The Council maintains a "Travel Store" at 680 Beach Street, next to the Cannery in San Francisco, where you can purchase a hostel pass, travel books and sleep sacks. For more information, call them at 415-771-4646.

When planning a hostel trip, it's a good idea to call the hostel you'll be staying at to make a reservation well in advance. Walk-ins are often possible, but only if there are beds free. Rates run from $5.00 to $7.00 per night, and some hostels offer discounts to AYH members. Remember that most hostels don't open until late afternoon, usually 5:00, and lock up for the night around 11:00 p.m.

Montara/Pigeon Point: Exploring Lighthouse Country

Just 25 miles south of San Francisco, between Montara and Moss Beach, the Montara Fog Signal and Lighthouse Hostel provides a perfect setting for a seaside sojourn (reservations: 415-728-7177). Another 30 miles down the coast, Pigeon Point Lighthouse Hostel occupies the grounds of one of the tallest lighthouses in the United States (reservations: 415-879-0633). Why not combine the two for a three-day, 100-mile-plus coast tour?

Starting from Woodside, at the corner of Woodside Road (Highway 84) and Canada Road, you can purchase food, fill up on water and make a pit stop at Roberts Store. Once supplied, ride north on Canada, weaving in and out under Highway 280 and passing the Pulgas Water Temple. At Highway 92, turn left, then right onto Skyline Drive (a.k.a. Scenic Highway 35).

Skyline climbs up to Crystal Springs Road, where you can turn off the road into

The Pulgas Water Temple on Canada Road north of Woodside, is the terminus of the Hetch Hetchy Water System.

42

Sawyer Camp Trail on the left. This county recreational trail is shared by many runners, strollers, skaters and cyclists, so caution is in order. You'll certainly enjoy the beautiful surroundings of the Crystal Springs and San Andreas Reservoir watersheds.

At the end of its six-mile span, Sawyer Camp Trail climbs up to the reservoir's dam level and brings you out on Skyline again. Turn left, then left again at Larkspur. After you pass back under the freeway, you'll see another recreational trail, this one built by CalTrans. Much less populated than Sawyer Camp, this is a scenic bike path that eliminates an otherwise required detour on 280.

After exiting back onto Skyline, continue north to Sharp Park Boulevard, where you'll finally turn left for the downhill to Pacifica. This is a steep, curvy road that normally carries heavy traffic. Take care on your descent.

At the bottom cross Highway 1 and turn left on the frontage road. Make a left on Fairway Drive, right on Bradford Way, left on Westport and you'll be climbing up to the bike route for Highway 1. Make a right (I'd advise skipping the separate, extremely steep bike path and using the highway shoulder). From here you have seven miles of riding with the wind at your back to the village of Montara.

The hostel is about half a mile south of the Chart House restaurant on your right. Follow the hostel signs through the first parking lot and around past the lighthouse. The Chart House, by the way, is an excellent choice for replacing the calories you spent getting there.

The Montara Fog Signal and Light Station was originally built in 1875 to serve navigation off San Francisco Bay. The fog signal building, built in 1902, currently houses the hostel's community room. Separate bike storage is available in the "barn." There are also a volleyball court, private beach and outdoor hot tub on the premises. If you're intrigued by marine life, visit the tidepools at Fitzgerald Marine Reserve in Moss Beach. Or you can hike or mountain bike the trails of Montara State Park.

If you're not up to cooking your own breakfast the next morning in one of the hostel's two kitchens, head south on Highway 1 for about three and a half miles toward Princeton Harbor, where there's at least one deli serving fishermen and tourists daily. Or you can hang in there for another few miles to Half Moon Bay, where at least three bakeries beckon.

It's another ten miles south from Half Moon Bay to San Gregorio Beach. You can buy lunch, or almost anything else you need, at the General Store, less than a mile inland at the corner of Highway 84 and Stage Road.

Still not hungry? Hang on for five more miles to Pescadero. Duarte's Tavern, a couple miles east on Stage Road off Pescadero Road, offers artichoke soup, excellent omelets and homemade fruit pies.

About five miles further down Highway 1, you'll come to Pigeon Point Lighthouse and your second hostel stopover. Once Coast Guard family residences, each of the three bungalows has its own kitchen, and the former fog signal building serves as a recreation lounge and conference center. It's only a few more miles to Año Nuevo State Reserve and the elephant seal colony. You'll find more tidepools, but the elephant seals won't start arriving until at least December.

Your last day will begin with a ride back up north to Pescadero, so start early if you want to avoid heavy headwinds. At Pescadero Road, turn right and begin the climb up through the redwoods. In about eight miles, you'll come to the hamlet of Loma Mar, where once a great little vegetarian restaurant, the Blue-Eyed Goose, made an ideal stop. Alas, it no longer exists, so you should carry your own snacks from the store in Pescadero.

The climb up Haskins Hill is exposed and often grueling from this direction, but console yourself with the thought of the redwoods waiting on the other side. At Alpine Road, turn left for about a mile, then right onto Highway 84 (La Honda Road). You'll climb again, all the way up to Skyline. This is Skylonda, where you'll have to wait in line with the motorcyclists to buy snacks at the grocery store. Or sit with them for a meal at Alice's Restaurant across the street.

From Skylonda, it's all downhill on Highway 84 back to Woodside and the end of a fine introduction to hostel touring.

Sanborn Park: A Hideaway in the Redwoods

Operated by the Central California Council of AYH, the Sanborn Park Hostel (reservations: 408-741-9555) was originally built in 1908 by a San Jose judge named Welch as a hunting lodge. Known as Welch Lodge, it was purchased by Vernon Pick, the Colorado uranium multimillionaire. Fallen into disrepair, the lodge wound up in county possession in the late '50s. Ready to raze the building, Santa Clara County park officials finally agreed in 1979 to turn it over to AYH in exchange for its renovation.

And renovate it they did. Several bunkrooms provide dormitory-style accommodations, the kitchen is a dream to cook in, and an outdoor barbecue serves guests who prefer to dine al fresco.

If you're willing to do some serious climbing, you'll be treated to a serene environment at Sanborn Park, far from the hustle and bustle of Silicon Valley below. You'll have to carry your own food up the hill (no nearby stores here), although groups can have a barbecued chicken dinner prepared by AYH volunteers.

This route to the park offers some side trips through some of Santa Clara Valley's most intriguing neighborhoods, including Stanford University, Los Altos, Los Altos Hills and Stevens Creek County Park.

Start your 25-mile one-way trip at Stanford Shopping Center, at the corner of Quarry and Arboretum at the edge of the Stanford campus. Ride east on Arboretum and turn right on Palm Drive, then left on Campus

Drive. You'll pass through fraternity row before coming out at the East Campus Drive exit onto Junipero Serra Boulevard.

Make a left and continue onto Foothill Expressway after crossing Page Mill Road. The next light is Hillview Avenue. Turn right and climb up through part of the Stanford Industrial Park, descending into Los Altos Hills. Continue on Fremont, which bears left after passing the Town Hall.

At Burke, turn left and cross Foothill into downtown Los Altos. Turn right on First Street (the first light after Foothill) and cross San Antonio Road to Cuesta Drive. Make a right on Campbell and a left on Covington, then ride on to Grant Road.

Turn right on Grant and left on Foothill Expressway. Ride under Highway 280 and continue on Foothill Boulevard, which becomes Stevens Canyon Road. You'll climb up to Stevens Canyon Dam, then descend to Stevens Creek County Park to ride along the creek until you reach the fork in the road. Here you should bear left on Mount Eden Road for a nontrivial but short climb, then a fast descent to Pierce Road.

At Pierce gear down and turn right for another nontrivial climb and fast descent. You'll be at the intersection of Pierce and Highway 9 when you reach the bottom. Turn right and climb up to the signs for Saratoga Springs resort on the right. You'll see a left-turn lane just opposite the entrance.

Take the left turn onto Sanborn Road, where the climbing really becomes serious! Look for the hostel sign on the right, next to a group of mail boxes. Follow the signs into the hostel driveway, and the climbing is over — for today.

While you're at the hostel, you may want to tackle some more climbing on foot in Sanborn-Skyline County Park. Trails lead up to Skyline Boulevard, offering spectacular redwood forests and views of the valley below. Unfortunately, however, bicycles are strictly forbidden (thanks to the antics of some wahoos in the early '80s).

If you've had enough climbing for now, you can return to Stanford the way you came. However, if you're still game for some vertical challenge, continue up Highway 9 in the morning to Saratoga Gap, the intersection with Skyline Drive/Highway 35. Turn right on Skyline for a little over six miles to Page Mill Road. The descent down Page Mill requires much caution, for both the curves and the oncoming traffic. Stop to enjoy the views if you like. Or to take a hike in Los Trancos or Montebello Open Space Preserve (plenty of trails open to bikes!).

Just before Page Mill reaches Highway 280, turn left on Arastradero Road and ride three miles or so to Alpine Road. You can stop for refreshments at the Alpine Inn on your left. This historic landmark was once known as Risotti's, and the locals still refer to it as "Zots."

From Zots turn right on Alpine. At the bottom of the last hill, turn left at the light and right onto Willow Road. Stanford Shopping Center will soon be on your right, after passing Stanford Medical Center.

ROUTE SLIPS

Montara/Pigeon Point 3-Day Tour
Day 1: From Roberts Store, Highway 84 and Mountain Home Road in Woodside

TURN	ON	FOR
Left	Canada Road	8.0
Left	Highway 92	0.8
Right	Skyline Drive/Highway 35	1.6
Left	Sawyer Camp Trail	6.0
	At Crystal Springs Road	
Left	Skyline	1.0
Left	Larkspur	< 0.1
Continue	CalTrans Bike Trail	1.8
Left	Skyline	1.5
Left	Sharp Park Boulevard	2.2
	Cross Highway 1 at bottom	
Left	Frontage Road	0.3
	Becomes Fairway Drive	
Right	Bradford Way	0.1
Left	Westport	< 0.1
Right	Highway 1	7.0
Right	Montara Lighthouse Youth Hostel	

Day 2: From Montara Lighthouse Youth Hostel in Montara

Left	Highway 1	31.75
	...to Princeton	3.5
	...to Half Moon Bay	6.0
	...to San Gregorio	12.0
	...to Pescadero	5.0
	...to Pigeon Point Lighthouse	5.25
Right	Pigeon Point Lighthouse Youth Hostel	

Day 3: From Pigeon Point Lighthouse Youth Hostel

Left	Highway 1	5.25
Right	Pescadero Road	14.0
Left	Pescadero Road at Alpine Road Y	1.0
Right	La Honda Road/Highway 84	7.0
Continue	Woodside Road/Highway 84	6.25

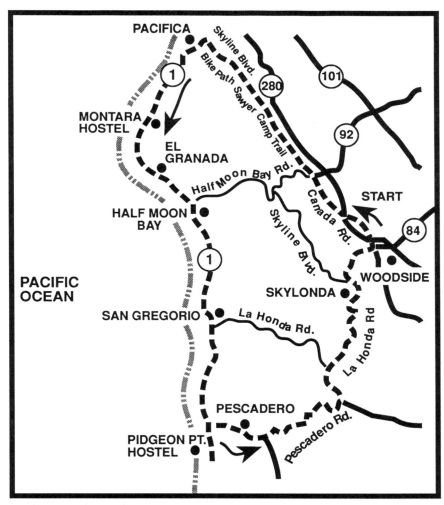

Sanborn Park Youth Hostel
Day 1: From Stanford Shopping Center, Quarry and Arboretum

Left	Arboretum	0.2
Right	Palm Drive	0.25
Left	Campus Drive	1.8
Left	Junipero Serra Boulevard	1.5
Continue	Foothill Expressway	0.6
Right	Hillview Avenue	0.6
Continue	Fremont Road	1.0

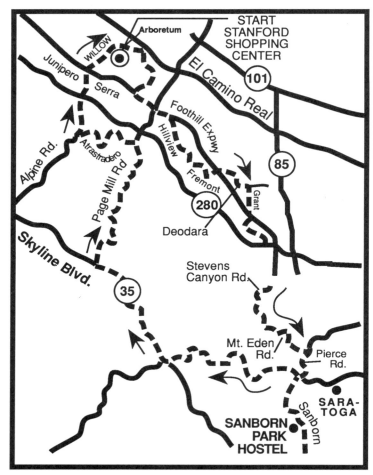

Left	Fremont	1.0
	At Los Altos Hills Town Hall	
Left	Burke Road	0.2
	Cross Foothill Expressway	
Right	First Street	1.0
	Becomes Cuesta Drive	
Right	Campbell	0.5
Left	Covington	2.5
Right	Grant Road	2.5
Left	Foothill	6.0
	Becomes Foothill Boulevard, then Stevens Canyon Road	

Left	Mt. Eden Road	2.25
Right	Pierce Road	1.0
Right	Highway 9	1.0
Left	Sanborn Road	1.0
Right	Sanborn Youth Hostel	

Day 2: From Sanborn Youth Hostel, off Sanborn Road in Sanborn-Skyline Park

Left	Sanborn Road	1.0
Left	Highway 9	5.0
Right	Skyline Drive/Highway 35	5.0
Right	Page Mill Road	8.5
Left	Arastradero Road	2.25
Right	Alpine Road	3.0
Left	Santa Cruz Avenue	0.2
Right	Willow Road	2.4
Left	Arboretum	0.1
Left	Quarry Road	
	To Stanford Shopping Center	

Año Nuevo's Elephant Seals
March 1989

Out beyond the rugged cliffs and surf-washed beaches of the southern San Francisco Peninsula lies Año Nuevo Island, once the northern end of Monterey Bay and long the site of a thriving elephant seal colony. About 15 years ago, when the colony got too big for the island, some of the bulls moved their broods to the neighboring beach. Well, one thing led to another, and today that beach, which is part of Año Nuevo State Reserve, is the largest elephant seal rookery on the mainland.

The breeding season starts in December, when the first bulls arrive, and lasts through March, when most of the adults take off for other waters. But many of the newly weaned pups stick around until early April. The latter part of breeding season is the best time to hop on your bike and ride over to the coast for a close, docent-led look at the little beggars.

Through March you'll need tickets (get them from Ticketron) to take part in the daily interpretive walks between 9:00 a.m. and 2:30 p.m. According to State Park Aide Jay Salter, weekends book up early, but it's often easy to pick up tickets for weekdays. Or simply wait until March is over and avoid the ticket scene entirely. There will still be docents hanging around to explain things, although they won't be leading formal tours.

Either way, be sure to take your lunch with you or buy it along the way at Skylonda or Pescadero; there are no snack bars at the reserve. And pack both a pair of lightweight walking shoes and a lock. Bikes can be ridden no further than the tour "staging area," about three quarters of a sandy mile from seal country.

The longer version of this ride is a 90-mile round-trip from Palo Alto over the Santa Cruz Mountains to Año Nuevo. If that's a bit much to take on this early in the season, you can split the effort into two days by spending the night at nearby Pigeon Point Lighthouse Hostel, just six miles north of Año Nuevo (reservations, 415-879-0633).

Another option is to cut the distance to a mere 71 miles by starting from Skylonda, at the intersection of Highway 35 (Skyline Boulevard) and Highway 84 (La Honda Road). This route lets you take the major downhill first and leave most of the serious climbing until after Año Nuevo.

Those who prefer their distance and hills on the lengthy side should start on Arastradero Road in Palo Alto and head south across Foothill Expressway toward the foothills. After passing under Interstate 280 and climbing the frontage road, turn left on Page Mill, then right back onto Arastradero for the two-mile roller-coaster ride to Portola Valley.

Make a left on Alpine for the gradual 1.2-mile climb to Portola Road, and turn right. Ride around the "loop" toward the Woodside turnoff, but just before you get there, make a left on Old La Honda Road. Here's where the real climbing begins! The site of many a club time trial, Old La Honda dishes out 3.3 miles of steep, narrow switchbacks on the way up to Skyline.

At the top, turn right on Skyline and shoot down the fast one-mile descent to Skylonda, where you can meet up with others who prefer the shorter route. There's food and water available at Skylonda Market on the northeast corner or at Alice's Restaurant on the northwest corner (if you have time for a sit-down meal).

Time to don your windbreaker for the six-mile descent to La Honda on Highway 84. Turn left from northbound Skyline (or right from Alice's or the Market) and enjoy the "coast." Before you know it, you'll be in La Honda looking for the left turn onto Pescadero Road toward San Mateo County's Sam McDonald and Memorial Parks.

Okay, fun's over. In about 1.2 miles, turn right on Pescadero Road and start climbing again, past Sam McDonald Park and over the top of Haskins Hill. Then it's down again, past the town of Pescadero and straight toward the ocean.

Turn left on Bean Hollow Road for a 2.5-mile bumpy but scenic ride behind the dunes. When you come out to Highway 1, make a cautious left turn into the coast traffic. It's ten more mostly rolling miles to Año Nuevo Reserve, on your right. Now it's time to rest and enjoy the antics of what may be the least lovely — but most lovable — creatures on the coast.

For the return trip, head north from Año Nuevo back toward Pescadero. In 5.6 miles, turn left on Gazos Creek Road, which becomes Cloverdale

Road in two miles and continues for almost six miles toward Pescadero.

Turn left onto Pescadero Road, then right on Stage Road to continue paralleling Highway 1. You'll pass through Pescadero, climb two big bumps, and drop down to San Gregorio. Here's where the long and short riders part company.

If you're on the long route, cross Highway 84 on Stage and take the short, winding climb up to Highway 1. Turn right for a super-scenic downhill overlooking Half Moon Bay, then right again onto Tunitas Creek Road just across the bridge. After about three miles, you'll enter the redwoods for a seriously nontrivial climb of about three more miles.

(Grant Petersen of *Roads to Ride* fame says the steepest part is 11.5%, but I'd swear it's steeper! He also says there's minimal traffic, but keep your eyes and ears peeled for the Sunday drivers who seem to have discovered this beautiful road in the last few years.)

When the worst is over, you'll still have three more miles of winding road to cover through more redwood forest before reaching Skyline. The fastest way back down to Bay level is straight across Skyline and down five-mile-long Kings Mountain Road. Be extra cautious along the narrow switchbacks; some are hairpin turns posted at 10 mph (and they mean it!).

At the bottom, you'll come out at Highway 84 in Woodside. Turn left, ride through town and make a right on Whiskey Hill Road. The next left will bring you out onto Sand Hill Road; climb the hill, cross Highway 280 and head down toward Menlo Park. At the intersection with Alpine and Santa Cruz, turn right, then get directly (but cautiously) into the left-turn lane for the turn onto Junipero Serra Boulevard, which becomes Foothill Expressway at Page Mill, only 1.3 miles from Arastradero Road.

If you started from Skylonda on the short route but don't want to miss the scenic redwoods on Tunitas Creek, go ahead and give it a try. You'll top out on Skyline just 7.5 miles north of Highway 84. Turn right, climb up to Skeggs Point and enjoy the mostly downhill return.

But if you're still in your right mind and prefer to skip the long Tunitas Creek climb, turn right up Highway 84 at San Gregorio. From La Honda, you'll be retracing your tracks for about four miles. Eleven miles up, you can still enjoy a change of scenery: Turn right onto the newly paved western section of Old La Honda Road for a five-mile climb up several forested switchbacks. It will bring you out on Skyline just a mile south of, and 400 feet above, Skylonda. Turn left and "shoot" the free-and-easy downhill back to your car!

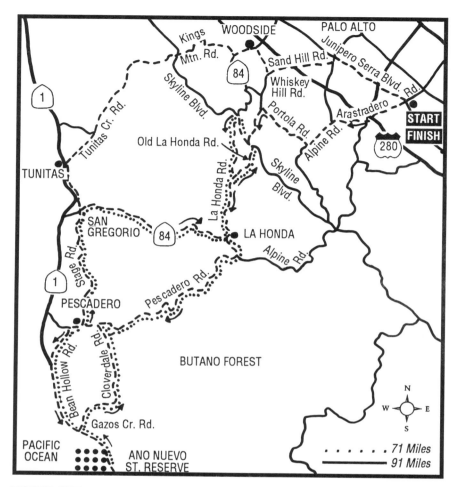

ROUTE SLIP

From Arastradero Road & Foothill Expressway in Palo Alto

TURN	ON	FOR
South	Arastradero	2.5
Left	Page Mill Road	0.25
Right	Arastradero	2.0
Left	Alpine Road	1.2
Right	Portola Road	3.0
Left	Old La Honda Road	3.3
Right	Skyline Boulevard/Highway 35	1.0
	Short option starts here at Skylonda	

Left	La Honda Road/Highway 84	6.0
Left	Pescadero Road	1.2
Right	Pescadero Road at Alpine	12.0
Left	Bean Hollow Road	2.5
Left	Highway 1	10.0
Right	Año Nuevo State Reserve	

Return:

Left	Highway 1	5.6
Right	Gazos Creek Road	2.0
Continue	Cloverdale Road	6.0
Left	Pescadero Road	0.5
Right	Stage Road	7.0
	Short option turns right on Highway 84 at 6.0 miles	
Right	Highway 1	1.5
Right	Tunitas Creek Road	9.0
	Turn right to return to Skylonda	
Continue	Kings Mountain Road	5.0
Left	Woodside Road/Highway 84	0.7
Right	Whiskey Hill Road	1.3
Left	Sand Hill Road	3.0
Right	Santa Cruz Avenue	0.1
Immed. Left	Junipero Serra	2.4
Continue	Foothill Expressway	1.3
	Exit at Arastradero Road	

High on History and Hills in Hillsborough
November 1988

Lisa loves hills.

When Lisa Dondick used to live in San Mateo, she didn't have to ride far to find the steep grades she craves. She just crossed El Camino Real into the town of Hillsborough, where an energetic cyclist can revel in a hill climber's paradise and discover a treasure trove of elaborate turn-of-the-century architecture as well.

Curious about the stories behind all those grand old estates, Lisa did some research into local history and came up with this vertical excursion into the past of one of the Peninsula's highest-per-capita-income, but least known, cities.

Her 20-mile route will take you up and down Hillsborough's hills and into its past, then bring you back down to the flats for a present-day, post-ride lunch. If you develop an appetite earlier in the ride, just head downhill toward the Bay, cross El Camino Real and then look for Burlingame Avenue.

Start from San Mateo's Central Park, off El Camino at North San Mateo Street and Fifth Avenue. You'll find restrooms and water there, but you may have a hard time finding an unmetered parking space. Try a side street and ride back.

Head north on San Mateo Drive across Fourth and Third and turn left on Baldwin for your first stop at St. Matthews Episcopal Church, on your left just before El Camino. This is the burial place of William Davis Howard, the founding father of Hillsborough. After making a fortune in hides and tallow, Howard procured for himself the last of the old Mexican land grants, nearly 6500 acres, in 1849. The Howard estate stretched from the Santa Cruz Mountains skyline to San Francisco Bay and included most of what is now Hillsborough, half of San Mateo, all of Burlingame and Coyote Point.

Cross El Camino into Hillsborough, continue on Baywood and make an immediate right onto DeSabla. This street is named for Eugene DeSabla, the founder of PG&E in 1905, who lived in the original Howard residence (which no longer exists).

Turn left on El Cerrito, which was the name of Howard's old estate, then left on Stonehedge and right on Uplands. At Rockridge, turn left and ride up to the gates of the Uplands Mansion. After Howard's death, his widow, Agnes Poett Howard, and her second husband, William's brother George, built this second Howard estate.

Continue your loop around Uplands on Sierra, turn left on Redwood and bear right to continue on Bridge. Turn left on Stonehedge to get back out to El Cerrito and make a left, then a right onto Poett. Continue on to Roblar and turn right, then left onto Severn for a short climb to Santa Inez Avenue. Turn left and continue on West Santa Inez. You'll pass number 233 on the left; it was Patti Hearst's family home when she was kidnapped, but it no longer houses any Hearsts.

At the Y, bear right to stay on West Santa Inez, then bear right again at the second Y onto Hillsborough Boulevard. After Hillsborough becomes Sharon Avenue, bear left onto Forestview and ride through the shade of the cypresses. Make a left onto Eucalyptus, then right to ride past the "Not a Through Road" sign into New Place. Beyond these gates is the Burlingame Country Club, the first exclusive club of its kind on the West Coast and now the oldest in the country. Check out the clubhouse, which was once one of the many Crocker mansions.

Turn around in the clubhouse parking lot and return to Eucalyptus, turn right and ride to San Raymundo. Make a right and then another right at the Y onto Pinehill.

It's time to gear down again as you begin the 2.5-mile climb to the

Caroland mansion.

Make a left on Pullman, named for Harriet Pullman Caroland, the railroad car heiress who, with her husband Francis, had the mansion built to entertain royalty attending the 1915 Panama Pacific International Exposition. A left on Craig brings you to the back of the mansion on your left. To see the front of the house, ride around the block and turn left on Ralston, then again on Remillard.

The Carolands gave one big party in the immense ballroom of this 92-room palace. Then they split up. After Francis died in 1923, Harriet closed down the house and the estate was subdivided. The mansion was to be razed but was saved by Countess Lillian Remillard Dandi, an heiress from Oakland. Although the JFKs were considering it for a "western White House," the countess ultimately died here in 1973, leaving the mansion to the city of Hillsborough for a cultural arts center. In 1988 it stood empty, unused by the city and unsold to developers, a grim reminder of the 1986 stabbing by the caretaker of two local girls, one of whom died.

By now you're almost to Skyline Boulevard and the highest point in your ride. Back at Ralston, turn right, then right again on Darrell. At Rowan Tree Lane make a left then a right on Skyline and an immediate right into the Nueva Learning Center, another former Crocker residence whose parking lot affords a nice view of the San Francisco International Airport. Make a loop around the one-way driveway back to Skyline and turn right. Make another right on Hillside at the sign to the Kohl Mansion and enjoy the great views of the Bay as you descend about a mile to the next Kohl Mansion sign at Alvarado. Turn left, cross Adeline and enter the gates of the Sisters of Mercy School.

The Kohl family's son Frederick was apparently a playboy type who "dallied" with the maid and received a bullet in his foot for his efforts! He remained in this house all his life, in constant fear that the maid would return to finish the job. After his death the Sisters of Mercy bought the estate and created a girls' prep school. Frederick's ghost has been "sighted" several times at the school, and three separate exorcisms apparently failed to banish him. Now, says Lisa, the sisters tell tales of "friendly old Freddie" looking after the girls, but she herself is sure "he was really an old lecher."

Ride back to Alvarado across Hillside Circle and turn right on Summit, then left on Easton Drive at Canyon. At Vancouver make a right on Jackling (you probably won't see the sign until you've made the turn). Continue straight onto Fagan at the Y and make an immediate right on Armsby. You're now climbing past the Bing Crosby home (Katherine still lived there in '88) behind the ivy-planted fence on your right.

Turn right at Carmelita, which becomes Oaks Drive, then left on McCreary and left on Forestview, back through the cypresses. Make a right on Eucalyptus, a left on Floribunda, a right on Pepper, and a left on

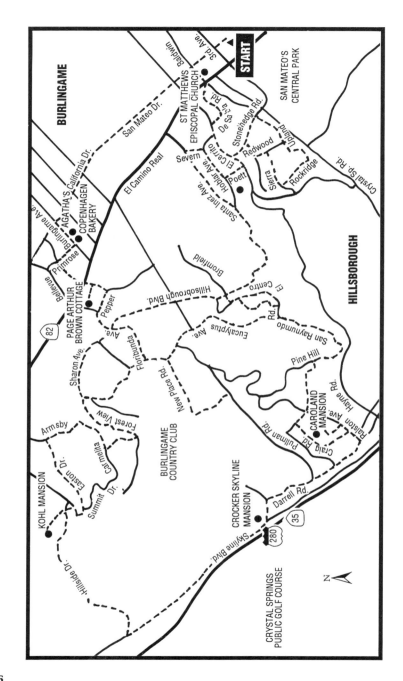

START

BURLINGAME

HILLSBOROUGH

SAN MATEO'S
CENTRAL PARK

ST MATTHEWS
EPISCOPAL CHURCH

3rd Ave.

Baldwin

De Sá Rd.

Stonehedge Rd.

Redwood

Upland

Crystal Sp. Rd.

Rockridge

Sierra

Severn

El Camino Real

San Mateo Dr.

California Dr.

AGATHA'S

COPENHAGEN
BAKERY

Burlingame Ave.

Primrose

Bellevue

El Cerrito

Poett

Hobart Ave.

Santa Inez Ave.

Bromfield

El Centro

San Raymundo

Eucalyptus Ave.

Rd.

Pine Hill

Hayne Rd.

CAROLAND
MANSION

Ralston Ave.

Craig Rd.

Pullman Rd.

PAGE ARTHUR
BROWN COTTAGE

82

Pepper

Ave.

Floribunda

New Place Rd.

Hillsborough Blvd.

Sharon Ave.

Forest View

Armsby

Easton Dr.

Carmelita

Summit Dr.

BURLINGAME
COUNTRY CLUB

KOHL MANSION

Hillside Dr.

CROCKER SKYLINE
MANSION

Skyline Blvd.

Darrell Rd.

280

35

CRYSTAL SPRINGS
PUBLIC GOLF COURSE

N

Bellevue and ride to Kammerer Court on your left. The last historical stop is at number 50, one of two summer rental cottages designed by renowned architect Page Arthur Brown and built in 1893.

Now it's back to Bellevue, across El Camino and right on Primrose to Burlingame Avenue for lunch. Lisa has recommended the scones at Agatha's, a tiny British-style tearoom on the corner, or just about anything at the Copenhagen Bakery. To return to San Mateo, turn right from Burlingame Avenue onto California Drive, which becomes North San Mateo Drive and ends at Central Park.

ROUTE SLIP

From Central Park, N. San Mateo Drive and Fifth Avenue in San Mateo

TURN	ON	FOR
North	San Mateo Drive	0.4
Left	Baldwin	0.15
	St. Matthews Episcopal Church	
Continue	Baywood	< 0.1
Immed. Right	DeSabla	0.4
Left	El Cerrito	0.25
Left	Stonehedge	0.3
Right	Uplands	0.25
Left	Rockridge	0.5
	Uplands Mansion	
Continue	Sierra	0.25
Left	Redwood	0.2
Bear Right	Bridge	0.1
Left	Stonehedge	0.1
Left	El Cerrito	0.1
Right	Poett	0.15
Right	Roblar	0.25
Left	Severn	0.1
Left	Santa Inez Avenue	0.25
Continue	West Santa Inez	0.5
Bear Right	West Santa Inez	0.25
Bear Right	Hillsborough Boulevard	1.5
	Becomes Sharon Avenue	
Bear Left	Forestview Avenue	0.25
Left	Eucalyptus	0.75
Right	New Place	1.25
	Burlingame Country Club/Crocker Mansion	
Right	Eucalyptus	1.0
Right	San Raymundo	0.5

Right	Pinehill	0.25
Left	Pullman	0.5
Left	Craig	0.5
	Caroland Mansion (back view)	
Right	Ralston	0.1
Left	Remillard	0.25
	Caroland Mansion (front view)	
Right	Ralston	0.25
Right	Darrell	1.0
Left	Rowan Tree Lane	0.1
Right	Skyline Boulevard	1.25
	Nueva Learning Center	
Right	Hillside	1.25
	Follow signs to Kohl Mansion	
Left	Alvarado	0.5
	Sisters of Mercy School/Kohl Mansion	
Reverse	On Alvarado	
Right	Summit	0.15
Left	Easton Drive	0.5
Right	Jackling (at Vancouver)	< 0.1
Continue	Fagan	0.1
Immed. Right	Armsby	0.25
	Crosby Estate	
Right	Carmelita	0.25
	Becomes Oaks Drive	
Left	McCreary	0.25
Left	Forestview	0.5
Right	Eucalyptus	0.5
Left	Floribunda	0.5
Right	Pepper	0.2
Left	Bellevue	0.15
Left	Kammerer Court	0.1
	1893 Brown Cottages	
Reverse	On Kammerer	
Right	Bellevue	0.25
Right	Primrose	0.25
Left	Burlingame Avenue	0.25
	Bakeries, tea, lunch	
Right	California Drive	1.5
	Becomes N. San Mateo Drive, to Central Park	

Cross-Training on the Peninsula

March 1987

Few things are more precious to the serious triathlete than time. Cross-training means hours on end in the pool and on the road, both afoot and on the bike. There just don't seem to be enough hours in a week to devote to all the training you really need.

The solution is to make every mile count. And that's what this ride is all about. It's only 27 miles long, but it's filled with sudden altitude changes — strenuous climbs and blazing descents that will help you build endurance, speed and bike handling skills. Do it repeatedly and your time will improve as you learn to attack the hills, both up and down.

While you're riding this route, you may notice its potential for endurance running. Long-distance runner Mimi St. Clair used to train on these hills when she lived in the area. After she moved south and became a certified bikie, she often returned to train with friends. Eventually she used the routes they ran to develop this ride for her bike club.

Oh yes, there's another plus: The ride is beautiful. Beginning in Woodside horse country, it winds its way through the scenic hills of Belmont, San Mateo, San Carlos and Redwood City. On the way it crosses the crest of the San Bruno mountains bordering the San Andreas Fault no less than three times!

Begin your ride at Woodside School, the former site of Woodside Town Hall on Highway 84, just west of Canada Road. Before taking off, you can stock up on bananas and use the upstairs bathroom at Roberts Store. If all you need is water for your bottle, use the faucet in the parking lot.

Once on the bike, ride north on Canada for seven miles, almost all the way to the Highway 92 interchange. As you approach Highway 92, look sharp on your right for the bike path paralleling the freeway up to Ralston Avenue. The only sign on the road is one that says: "MOTORIZED VEHICLES PROHIBITED," so it's easy to miss. Once you turn onto it, you'll see a San Mateo County recreational trail sign. The path climbs quickly, rising above the San Andreas Reservoir and crossing Highway 92 on an uphill bridge.

At the top, turn left onto Ralston beyond the traffic light. Once you've gone through the light, you'll be on Polhemus, charging downhill for a little less than a mile to De Anza. Make a right, then in one block a left onto Parrott Drive.

As Mimi says, it's "onward and upward" on Parrott, but not for long. The road soon dives downward, with many a twist and turn. The descents are steep, and it's easy to find yourself charging straight onto an unknown road off the route. About 2.5 miles down, Parrott actually divides, taking you onto a strange street on the right for about 75 yards, then jogging left

Ralston Bike Path

again for another quarter to half mile.

At the bottom, turn right on Alameda de las Pulgas, the "Avenue of the Fleas" (giving us some idea of the problems encountered by the early Spanish explorers). Don't be fooled by the gently rolling terrain at the beginning. You'll actually have some 2.5 miles of thigh burning to put in before you reach the crest at Cipriani.

If you don't turn right at Cipriani, you'll find yourself going down what I refer to as the Alameda Wall! It's a sheer one-block drop that's only about half a lane wide, but serves two-way traffic — not exactly healthy territory for a bicycle!

Cipriani's another twisty-turny, up-and-down road, but it only lasts about two-thirds of a mile, bringing you back to Ralston. Make a right and ride about a mile to Hallmark, at the traffic light. Turn left here and begin a roller-coaster ride that crests at Hallmark Park.

Uphill on your right you'll see the beginning of a cross-country running course. Actually, according to Mimi, there are several courses, the longest one about two miles and the toughest about one mile. If you plan to leave your bike and do some foot training, keep in mind that cross-country meets are often held here, and it can get crowded. The views of the Bay and the city are magnificent, though.

Back on the road, you'll parallel the running trails briefly, then charge downhill to a barrier where only "feet and bike wheels can go," as Mimi puts it. Use the sidewalk on either side to cross from Hallmark to Crestview, and look up! There's the first of two real thigh burners that together last about three quarters of a mile to the crest, and the view, which stretches from the Redwood City salt flats back behind you to the San Francisco skyline.

Turning forward again, it's a mile and a quarter to Edgewood Road at the bottom, so let 'er rip! At Edgewood, turn right for about a third of a mile, then make another right onto Cordilleras, a pleasant — but bumpy — parallel to Edgewood that will bring you into Redwood City. Make a right on Canyon Road, then left on Highland, for one block, to Jefferson.

Turn right on Jefferson and wind around a bit to where it divides off from Farm Hill Boulevard. Be sure you make the sharp right to stay on Jefferson. The climb proceeds for about a mile to Upper Emerald Lake, and tops out in about another third of a mile. Then it's a little over a mile down to Canada Road, where you'll turn left to return to Woodside.

Now, if you've finished in less than two hours, you'll not only have worked up to faster riding time, but you may just have some extra time for a swim, run or weight session today!

ROUTE SLIP

From Woodside School on Highway 84 in Woodside

TURN	ON	FOR
Left	Woodside Road/Highway 84	0.25
Left	Canada Road	7.0
Right	Bike path to Ralston Avenue	
	Just before Highway 92 interchange	
Left	Ralston Avenue	1.0
	Becomes Polhemus Road	
Left	Parrott Drive	3.0
	In 2.5 miles, jog right/left to stay on Parrott	
Right	Alameda de las Pulgas	3.25
Right	Cipriani Boulevard	0.7
Right	Ralston	1.0
Left	Hallmark Drive	1.25
	Through barrier	
Continue	Crestview Drive	2.0
Right	Edgewood Road	0.3
Right	Cordilleras Road	0.75
Right	Canyon Road	0.6
Left	Highland Avenue	< 0.1
Right	Jefferson Avenue	0.25

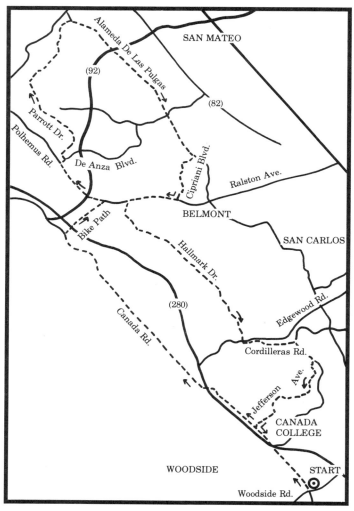

Right	Jefferson	2.3
	At Farm Hill Boulevard	
Left	Canada	1.5
Right	Woodside Road/Highway 84	0.25
	To Woodside School	

My Favorite Mountain Bike Ride: Crazy Pete Road

March 1988

This ride originally appeared as "Great Mountain Bike Fun on the Peninsula."

At last it can be told! It's been over five years since Chuck Guzis introduced me to this fantastic, mostly off-road loop from Portola Valley up Crazy Pete Road to Skyline and back down again. Every time I've ridden it since, I've wanted to share it with *California Bicyclist* readers. But the route passed through private property.

Technically there's nothing wrong with that. Section 846 of the State Civil Code releases private property owners from liability when folks enter their land for "recreational purposes." And in this case, we were hardly disturbing anyone as we followed an old jeep track through open range between two Midpeninsula Regional Open Space Preserves.

Still, I was unwilling to invite every mountain biker in the Bay Area onto someone else's real estate. But now the property has become part of the Midpeninsula Open Space District, and legal for bicycles! So here it is: a 15-mile loop chock full of aerobic workouts, technical challenges and fabulous scenery.

Our traditional starting spot is at the Alpine Inn (formerly Risotti's, which is why we call it "Zots"). Located at the corner of Arastradero and Alpine roads in Portola Valley, Zots is a beer-and-wine bar that serves up giant greasy hamburgers and fries. After 11:00 a.m. on any given day, you'll find the parking lot filled with a fascinating cross-section of conveyances, from Mercedes and BMWs to Harley-Davidsons to horses. And the beer garden in the rear is usually lined with bicycles.

Start your ride by pedaling through Risotti's upper dirt parking lot to the far right-hand corner. Ride up the little "bump" to the paved bike path along Alpine, turn left and follow it to Creek Park Drive. Exit onto Alpine here, turn left and keep riding south in the bike lane.

You'll see lots of signs warning that the pavement ends in a couple of miles. Don't believe it. Last year new pavement was laid all the way up to Joaquin Road, the only access to Los Trancos Woods from this side of Page Mill Road. Just beyond Joaquin, you'll come to a pipe gate, and good, honest dirt.

Hoist your bike over or through the gate, or ride up the driveway to the left and down the single track onto the dirt road. Then just keep chugging up Alpine for another mile and a half. If it's been raining lately, you'll have plenty of mud to slog through, but take heart. The runoff seems to collect at the bottom of dirt Alpine, while it remains relatively dry further up.

In 1988, you would have had some slides to negotiate. The first and

63

worst was just after the switchback beyond the gate. The portage was steep and slippery. Up the road a piece were two more slides in a direct link, sidestepped by single track on the right edge. A little tricky for acrophobics like me, it was still negotiable.

(All those slides are now gone, thanks to the regrading of dirt Alpine Road. How long they remain gone depends on how well the most recent drought is broken, and how soon!)

The turnoff to Crazy Pete Road is about a mile beyond where the last slide was. Keep your eyes peeled for a fence blocking a short single track up to an oak grove on the right, just before a sharp hairpin turn to the left. Once you could have climbed to the grove and, if the weather was fair, you'd be rewarded with a lookout that included part of the San Francisco skyline and Mount Tam. Now the area is under rehabilitation, but it's still okay to walk up the track.

Just beyond the fence, look for the Open Space boundary sign on the right, marking yet another steep, short single track. This is an entrance to Coal Creek Preserve, and the connection to Crazy Pete Road. Miss it and you'll continue all the way up to another pipe gate at Page Mill Road, a mile below Skyline.

The single track will lead you to a hiker stile, over which you'll have to carry your bike. Then you'll continue climbing to a footbridge, followed by a quick downhill on single track. You'll soon make up for it, though, as you begin climbing toward Skyline on Crazy Pete Road (named for Peter Coutts, a French immigrant who got rich by grabbing up much of the land surrounding Stanford University before the turn of the century).

About halfway up you'll come to a Y. Bear left to continue up Crazy Pete on dirt road. Go right and you'll climb on single track trail with forgiving gradients and switchbacks, making this section a perfect opportunity to get in some single tracking practice.

Road and trail meet again just beyond a big fallen log. Beyond the pipe gate, the climbing gets downright serious as the dirt road changes to the paved driveway. That driveway always gets me; as of this original writing, I've cleaned it exactly once. If you're used to slogging up steep hills and don't resent having to do it on a fat-tire bike, you'll probably detest it a bit less than I do.

At the top, you'll come out on Skyline Drive (Highway 35). Turn right and ride the 3.8 miles to Windy Hill. It's mostly downhill, with a couple of minor bumps. If your bike's picked up a lot of mud on the way up, you'll shed it on this section!

Pass the Windy Hill Open Space parking lot and picnic area and continue to the north side of the hill. Look for a hiker stile on the right. On the other side of the stile, you might see some "no bikes" signs. These signs refer to the trail leading back over the hill to the main parking lot. Do not

Several years ago, "dirt Alpine" Road was littered with landslides. This one was a serious portage.

ride in that direction! Instead, take the trail over the near edge of the hill.

As soon as you crest this low edge, you'll see there's no place left to go but DOWN! Before you take the plunge, check out your surroundings. In spring the grass around you will be so high, you'll barely be able to see the trail. But if you arrive after the grass has been cut, you'll be riding through stubble.

Below the first downhill pitch, there used to be a pipe spouting water just to the left of the trail. It was good water, fresh from an artesian well that ran year round. Alas, not long after the Open Space District acquired this land, they plowed the whole thing under.

The jeep track continues — fast! — down to where it merges with a wide hard-pack trail. Your view of this entire descent is clear from the ridge all the way down. If any hikers or horses are on the trail, you'll see them well in advance of an encounter. So you'll have plenty of time to remember to yield right of way.

Soon you'll come to another Y, and another choice. To the left you'll have a flat exit from Coal Creek running behind the Sequoias Convalescent Hospital and intersecting with Portola Road. From here, turn right on Portola, then left on Alpine to return to the Alpine Inn.

But if you're looking for more adventure, choose the right fork for a super crossing of little-known Madera Creek. You'll zip downhill a bit more, over some small rock outcroppings, then suddenly you'll be at the creek's edge. Unless the water is unusually high, the ford is an easy one.

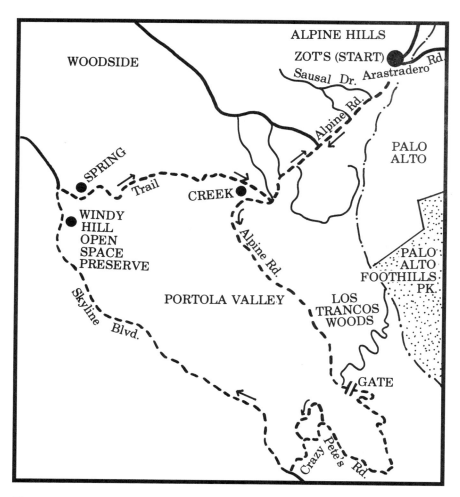

Just gear all the way down and keep pedaling!

In just a few more crank turns you'll reach the trailhead on Alpine Road, just above Willowbrook. Turn left and take the paved downhill back to Zots. Time to relax in the beer garden with a brew or a coke, maybe a burger and some fries, and a few friends.

ROUTE SLIP

From Alpine Inn, corner of Arastradero and Alpine Roads in Portola Valley

TURN	ON	FOR
Left	Through parking lot	
Right/Left	Onto Bike Path	
Right	At Creek Park Drive	
Left	Alpine Road	3.5
Continue	"Dirt" Alpine beyond gate	1.5
Right	Into Coal Creek Preserve	
Left	At Y onto Crazy Pete Road	

Optional Single Track:

Right	At Y	
Left	At log across trail	
Right	Onto Crazy Pete Road	
Right	Skyline Drive/Highway 35	3.8
Right	Trailhead on NORTH side of Windy Hill	
	Do not take trails signed "No Bikes!"	
Left	At Y behind Convalescent Hospital	
Right	Portola Road	0.5
Left	Alpine Road	1.25

Optional Creek Crossing:

Right	At Y behind Convalescent Hospital	
	Descend switchbacks and cross Madera Creek	
Left	Alpine Road	2.0

All:

Right	Arastradero Road	
	Into Zots	

A Civic Art Lover's Tour of Stanford

December 1988

The holidays are here again. The kids are out of school. Out-of-town relatives come to visit. What better time to gather everybody together for a short, easy tour both Aunt Emma and your eight-year-old might enjoy?

This tour of Stanford University is just the ticket. In no more than three to four miles, you'll discover a vast collection of outdoor sculpture to stop and admire. And if that's not enough reason for lots of stops, you'll also need to figure out where you are on the map.

Unless you're a Stanford student, alum, prof or staff member, you will get lost. It's easy, even with the best maps and directions. But all the stops on this tour are within shouting distance of each other, so you won't wander far. If you do, you may just discover another piece of art or architecture to "ooh and aah" over.

Stanford is a cycling campus. Almost everyone rides a bike of some kind or other, and bike paths outnumber roads. Some go where motor traffic can't, while others parallel roads but often disappear or go off in another direction without warning. Pedal traffic can be a bit chaotic during classes and on fair-weather weekends, but should be relatively light during Christmas vacation.

For the convenience of those who drive to the start, this route begins at Stanford Shopping Center's parking lot. It may be crowded this time of year, but, unlike the campus lots, it's free. Besides, you're almost sure to find a space if you look in the northeast corner of the quadrant, off Quarry Road and close to El Camino Real.

You can drive there from Highway 280 toward Menlo Park on Alpine Road. Turn left at Santa Cruz Avenue, right on Willow Road. Just beyond the Medical Center, turn right on Arboretum, left on Quarry and left into the parking lot.

If you must have your daily exercise fix, you can ride from the South Bay to Foothill Expressway and head north. Cross Page Mill Road to continue on Junipero Serra Boulevard, bear right on Santa Cruz at Alpine and follow the same directions to Stanford. From the north, take Alameda de las Pulgas, continue on Santa Cruz and turn left on Willow. From the Dumbarton Bridge, take University through downtown Palo Alto, cross under El Camino, continue on Palm Drive and turn right on Arboretum.

Everybody together now? Pedal south on Quarry and turn left on Arboretum. Cross Palm and turn right on Galvez at the Y. Cross Campus Drive and make a right onto Memorial Way. Go through the barriers onto the sidewalk and around the Graduate School of Business building to the Oval, the home of the "Pillars of Hercules" by Dmitri Hadzi.

Continue south on the bike path across Serra Street to the cluster of

Approaching the "Gates of Hell," Rodin Sculpture Garden.

buildings just west of Hoover Tower. In Dorman Grove, in front of the Stanford Art Gallery, you'll find "Retrofutée," which reminds me of a cluster of mushrooms poking out into the sunshine in an otherwise dark forest.

Next door to the Gallery you'll find the Cummings Art Building. First you'll probably spot "Facade" by Arnaldo Pomodoro, next to the front door. Look to your left and you'll see "Oiseau" by Joan Miro down in the courtyard. As you pedal away toward Green Library, you'll see "Large Torso: Arch" by Henry Moore on the left.

Pass Green on your left and turn left toward Meyer Library and Rodin's "The Thinker." The last privately owned cast of this famous statue, it was the most recent addition to Stanford's Outdoor Art program in 1988.

By now you've probably heard the clock chimes ringing every quarter hour and wondered where they were. Ride back out to the bike path, turn left and you'll see The Clock enclosed in glass. It's a complete restoration of a pre-1906 original. (This will undoubtedly be voted favorite stop by all pre-adolescent model makers and mechanical engineers!)

From The Clock, head around the near side of the Placement Center toward the Bookstore and you'll see "Mozart" by Kenneth Snelson glinting in the sun. Ride the path circling it to catch the different reflections off the stainless steel tubes. Then continue past the Bookstore to the Law School for a view of "The Falcon" by Alexander Calder. Then turn right back toward the Bookstore and Post Office, pick up the road past the Braun Music Center and ride over to Kresge Auditorium and "Vanguard," sculpted by Bruce Beasley.

Now it's time to turn around and head back north. Cut around the Post

Office, between the Bookstore and the Old Union, for a glimpse of White Plaza and the White Memorial Fountain. The day I took this tour in late October, a bicycle rested serenely on top of the fountain, apparently some undergraduate's attempt to replace the water that used to surge up there during non-drought days.

If you're ready for a break, continue straight to Tressider Union, where you can make a pit stop, get a snack or drink and relax on the terrace or patio. There's a snack shop, a quick-serve pizza window and a full-scale cafeteria to choose from.

Once refreshed, ride back to White Plaza, turn right and head back

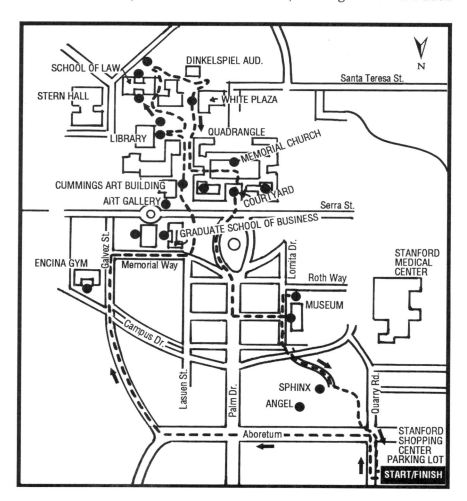

along the bike path past The Clock. Turn left through the wrought iron gates opposite Green Library into The Quad and pull up to admire the colorful friezes on Memorial Church and the bas-relief designs on the archways to Memorial Courtyard. All of this area may still be undergoing restoration to its condition before the 1989 Loma Prieta earthquake.

Ride on out of the courtyard (if you can, or carry your bike if you must) and circle around the Oval to Palm Drive. Follow the sign to the Stanford Museum by turning left on Museum Way. In front of the museum building you'll see another Pomodoro, "Cube," directly in front of a classical statue of "Menander," who seems to be puzzling over why his personal space has been invaded by that big hunk of bronze!

Make a left on Lomita and dismount at the Rodin Sculpture Garden. You may want to park your bike and spend some extra time here. From "The Gates of Hell" to "The Burghers of Calais," there's a universe of sight and touch to explore, all turned out by the hand of the great master.

Finally, turn left on Lomita, ride out to Campus Drive and jog left, then right, at the sign for Lomita. You'll find yourself on a poorly maintained bike path to the Stanford Family Mausoleum. The crypt is surrounded by sphinxes and guarded a little further up the path by William Wetmore Story's "Angel of Grief."

Continue up the bike path and you'll be at the corner of Quarry and Arboretum. Take care crossing to the Shopping Center; you may not be visible to traffic on either side of the street.

ROUTE SLIP

All distances are less than half a mile.

From Stanford Shopping Center, Quarry & Arboretum Roads

TURN	ON
South	Quarry Road
Left	Arboretum Road
Right	Galvez Street
Right	Memorial Way
	Ride through barriers to bike path
Bear left	To the Oval
	Pillars of Hercules
Continue	Bike path to Dorman Grove & Art Gallery
	Retrofutée, Façade, Oiseau
Continue	To Green Library
	Large Torso: Arch
Left	To Meyer Library
	The Thinker
Left	On bike path to The Clock

Left	Around Placement Center toward Bookstore
	Mozart
Continue	Past Bookstore to Law School
	The Falcon
Right	To Kresge Auditorium
	Vanguard
Reverse	Between Bookstore and Old Union
Left	Into the Quad
Circle	To Palm Drive
Left	Museum Way
	Cube, Menander
Left	Lomita
	Rodin Sculpture Garden
Left	Lomita
Left	Campus
Immed. Right	Onto bike path at Lomita sign
	Stanford Family Mausoleum, Angel of Grief
Continue	Bike path to Arboretum and Stanford Shopping Center

Christmas Tree Lane

December 1984

This ride originally appeared as "Holiday Meanderings on the Peninsula."

This time of year a short bike tour can become a special occasion for shared experiences. Try meandering along a stream, watching the fog drift above the trees. Stop to sip a steaming cup of hot chocolate at a corner coffee shop, or to watch artisans put finishing touches on gifts at what could be a replica of Santa's workshop. And top off the day with a short tour of holiday lights and decorations.

You can combine all these treats in less than 15 miles on a loop through Menlo Park and Palo Alto. The flat terrain makes it easy for the whole family to enjoy together, especially since frequent stops are almost essential. Be sure to bring locks, bike lights and plenty of warm clothing.

Your ultimate destination will be "Christmas Tree Lane," a two-block stretch of Fulton Street between Embarcadero Road and Seale Street in Palo Alto. Each year the residents put up elaborate lights and decorations, a tradition handed down for decades. When families move out, their part of Christmas Tree Lane is sold with the house, keeping continuity since many of the homes here were new in the 1950s.

Start at the Palo Alto Community Cultural Center at the corner of Newell and Embarcadero. It's just a few blocks from Fulton, and there's plenty of parking there and at the library next door. Ride north on Newell, away from Embarcadero, toward Hamilton Avenue.

Turn left on Hamilton for a short tour of Old Palo Alto, then right on Chaucer to cross San Francisquito Creek into Menlo Park. Continue on Pope, bearing right then left on the circle to stay on the route. Make a left at Gilbert, then another left on Marmona and a right on Blackburn.

At Willow, turn left with caution, since this a major artery from the Dumbarton Bridge to Middlefield Road. Cross Middlefield at the light and turn right on Laurel Street, which takes you past the Menlo Park Rec Center to a left on Ravenswood, another major artery to El Camino.

To avoid the traffic turning on El Camino, turn right on Merrill just before the light, then left on Santa Cruz Avenue. Continue up Santa Cruz across El Camino to the corner of University Avenue; Peet's Coffee Shop sits on the left-hand corner.

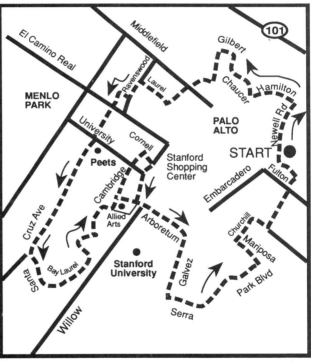

At Peet's you'll find the finest coffees, teas and cocoas to drink on the premises or take home (great gifts!). Stop for a cup if you like. You'll enjoy the people-watching through the glass-windowed walls.

Back on your bikes again, continue west on Santa Cruz and follow it to the left towards Stanford University. The first left turn after bearing left is Oakdell Drive. Take it and turn right on Oak Knoll, which will also bear left, after which you make a right on Bay Laurel to begin meandering along San Francisquito Creek.

Where Bay Laurel temporarily dead ends, turn left on Allbrandon Way, then right on Oak Avenue and right on Ambar Way to pick it up again. Follow the creek, jogging right on San Mateo, then left back on Bay Laurel. At Arbor Drive, turn right for another stop at Allied Arts Guild. It's behind the adobe walls on your right.

Here local artisans maintain tiny shops tucked into buildings surrounding flower and herb gardens. You'll find unique gifts and perhaps see how some are made. If Santa's workshop isn't something like this, it should be.

The Stanford Children's Hospital Auxiliary runs a gift shop at Allied Arts, as well as a tearoom where group lunches are served. If you're touring in a group, you might want to make reservations for the tearoom, but be warned: make them far in advance! Open dates are few and far between. The phone number is 415-324-2588.

From Allied Arts, turn right, then left on Creek Drive for half a mile. By now, if the weather is typical for December, you've probably had your fill of foggy scenery, so make a left on Cornell, away from the creek. Turn left on Cambridge, right on Arbor, and left at Bay Laurel. At San Mateo, turn left again and take the bike bridge over the creek.

Take the left fork in the bike path, then turn left on Willow Road. Make a right on Arboretum at Stanford Shopping Center and ride through the west end of the Stanford campus. Turn right on Galvez, left on Campus Drive and left on Serra to cross El Camino. Continue on Park Boulevard and make a left through the barrier that permits bikes to cut short of Peers Park into the tiny community of Southgate. Follow the road to the right onto Mariposa and turn right on Churchill, crossing the SP railroad tracks at the light.

Make a right onto Bryant and in four blocks turn left on Seale. After crossing Middlefield, turn left on Fulton and you'll be on Christmas Tree Lane, just two blocks from Embarcadero. If it's not twilight yet, you may want to take a supper or snack break at Town & Country Village, at the corner of El Camino and Embarcadero. If it's after dusk, though, get out your bike lights and tour the sights. You may want to dismount and walk the two blocks if the traffic is heavy (it nearly always is).

To avoid riding on Embarcadero after dark, turn around on Christmas Tree Lane for a second look and ride back to Seale. Turn left, then left again on Newell. You'll now be able to cross Embarcadero with a traffic light and return to the Cultural Center across the street.

ROUTE SLIP

From the Palo Alto Cultural Center, Newell & Embarcadero

TURN	ON	FOR
Right	Newell	0.6
Left	Hamilton	0.6
Right	Chaucer	0.4
	Becomes Pope; bear right around circle	
Left	Gilbert	0.1

74

Left	Marmona	.25
Right	Blackburn	0.1
Left	Willow	0.5
Right	Laurel	0.5
Left	Ravenswood	0.2
Right	Merrill	0.1
Left	Santa Cruz Avenue	1.75
Left	Santa Cruz Avenue at Avy	0.25
Left	Oakdell Drive	0.1
Right	Oak Knoll Lane	0.25
Right	Bay Laurel	0.25
Left	Allbrandon Way	0.1
Right	Oak Avenue	0.1
Right	Ambar	0.15
Left	Bay Laurel	0.5
	Jog right on San Mateo, left on Bay Laurel	
Right	Arbor	0.2
	Allied Arts on right	
Left	Creek Drive	0.75
Left	Cornell	0.2
Left	Cambridge	0.4
Right	Arbor	0.1
Left	Bay Laurel	0.2
Left	San Mateo over Bike Bridge	0.25
	Bear left toward Willow	
Left	Willow Road	0.3
Right	Arboretum	0.7
Right	Galvez	0.25
Left	Campus	0.5
Left	Serra	0.4
Continue	Park Boulevard	0.1
Left	At barrier at Peers Park	
Right	Mariposa	0.3
Right	Churchill	0.25
Right	Bryant	0.3
Left	Seale	0.4
Left	Fulton	0.3
	Christmas Tree Lane	
Reverse	At end of Fulton	0.3
Left	Seale	0.4
Left	Newell	0.2
Right	Palo Alto Cultural Center	

Santa Cruz Mountain Wineries
July 1990

There's something special about wine tasting by bike. You log your miles getting there, and then get an extra reward...a sip or two of a newly discovered vintage.

These two wineries, at opposite ends of California Scenic Highway 35 (also known as Skyline Drive), are from rides led by Hy Tran for Western Wheelers. Each offers a pleasant picnic area and welcomes cyclists, a state of mind you don't generally encounter in more congested wine regions up north. On the other hand, keep in mind that both are strenuous rides, with long, often steep climbs to tackle both before and after tasting.

Obester Winery in Half Moon Bay is a 63-mile round-trip from Palo

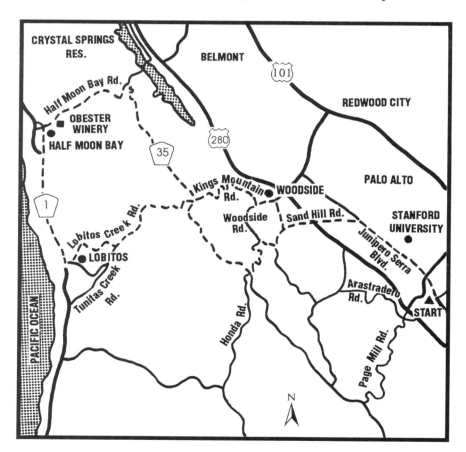

Alto. From Woodside, take Canada Road to the Skyline/Highway 92 intersection and turn left. The climb's not an overly difficult one, but the traffic on the descent can be a little unnerving. Obester is on the left about 1.5 miles before you reach town. Hy suggests trying the chenin blanc; "it's light," he says, "but not sweet like you'd expect a chenin blanc to be."

David Bruce Winery is nestled on Bear Creek Road between the southern end of Skyline and Summit Road. On this 70-mile ride the easiest approach is from Skyline going south; turn right down Bear Creek and right into the winery. Hy says they're known for "robust" reds; be sure to try the petite sirah. Then continue down Bear Creek to Boulder Creek and return to Skyline on the easier grades of Highway 9. Just remember to use extra post-tasting caution on the steep downhill!

A few more rules of thumb for riding and imbibing: Put off tasting when you first arrive, and let your pulse settle down to its resting rate. Try to eat lunch, or at least a nutritious snack, before you belly up to the tasting bar. And when you do, take just a few sips of each sample, clearing your palate with plenty of water and breadsticks in between to help counter the effects of the alcohol.

ROUTE SLIPS

Obester Winery, Half Moon Bay
From Gunn High School, Foothill Expressway and Arastradero Road, Palo Alto

TURN	ON	FOR
Right	Arastradero Road	0.2
Right	Foothill Expressway	1.0
Continue	Junipero Serra	2.5
Right	Alpine Road	0.1
Immed. Left	Sand Hill Road	3.0
Right	Whiskey Hill Road	1.6
Left	Woodside Road/Highway 84	0.9
	Food, water, restrooms at Roberts Store	
Right	Kings Mountain Road	5.0
Right	Skyline Drive/Highway 35	7.0
Left	Highway 92	3.5
Left	Obester Winery	
	Ride on into Half Moon Bay to buy food	

Return:

Left	Highway 92	1.5
Left	Main Street	1.5
Left	Highway 1	5.0
Left	Verde/Lobitos Creek	4.2

Left	Tunitas Creek	5.3
Right	Skyline/35	5.5
Left	Highway 84	3.5
	Sharp hairpin turn at bottom!	
Right	Portola Road	1.0
	To Sand Hill Road	
Right	Portola	4.3
Left	Alpine Road	1.3
Right	Arastradero	2.5
Left	Page Mill Road	.25
Right	Arastradero	2.2
Left	Gunn High School	

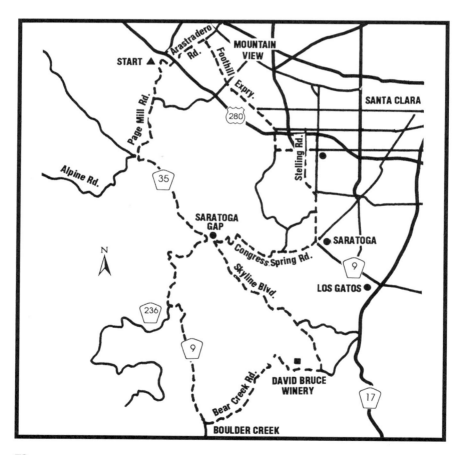

David Bruce Winery, Boulder Creek
From Gunn High School

TURN	ON	FOR
Right	Arastradero Road	2.2
Left	Page Mill Road	9.0
Left	Skyline Drive/Highway 35	16.8
	Water at fire station just before Highway 9 junction	
Right	Bear Creek Road	0.2
Right	David Bruce Winery	
Return:		
Right	Bear Creek Road	13.0
	Steep descent to Boulder Creek (check out bakery)!	
Right	Highway 9	13.7
	Seemingly endless climb to Saratoga Gap	
Continue	Highway 9	7.2
	More bakeries in Saratoga	
Left	Saratoga-Sunnyvale Road	2.0
Left	Prospect Road	0.4
Right	Stelling Road	3.0
Left	Homestead Road	1.5
Right	Foothill Expressway	6.0
Right	Arastradero	0.2
Left	Gunn High School	

Killer Hills of the Peninsula
September 1985

Two months ago, when last I wrote of killer hills, I picked two east of San Francisco Bay. If Mt. Diablo and Cantelowe Road weren't enough for you, here are two more, to be found west of San Francisco Bay and not to be taken lightly.

To refresh your memory, a "killer hill" is one that represents more threat than challenge when it appears on the horizon. Some may call it a "wall," others a "nontrivial climb." But after all the horror stories, a killer hill is no more than what you yourself make it. Get out there and ride that killer a few times, and before you know it, it won't seem quite so devastating anymore.

For the sake of convenience, I've designated the "Peninsula" as reaching all the way down to Saratoga. There are several reasons for my abominable geography. Among them is the fact that I'm more familiar with the northern end of Santa Clara County than I am with the northern parts of San Mateo County. Besides, I've already covered prime candidate Tunitas Creek Road, from Highway 1 near Half Moon Bay up to Skyline Boulevard, in a previous ride.

But the most important reason for my dragging the region south a ways is that I can now include the great granddaddy of killer hills. This month I get to introduce you to Redwood Gulch Road.

I hasten to add that there are plenty of other killers available for Peninsula hill climbers to tackle. Try Golden Oak off Alpine in Portola Valley. (If you start to sag, you can turn off on one of the side roads and still have a killer climb to finish!) Then there's Altamont Road up from Foothill College and on to Page Mill Road, or Moody Road from the same intersection to even farther up Page Mill.

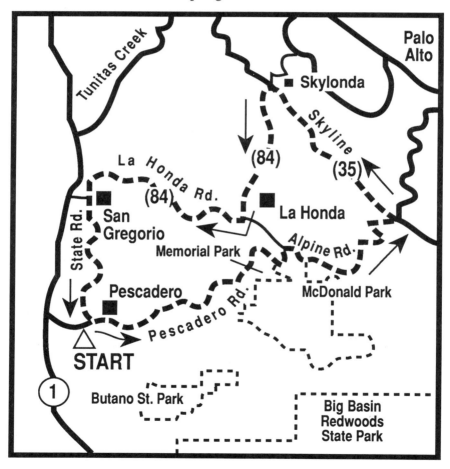

The Alpine Climb

How about a 2000-foot climb in just under seven miles, immediately after two miles of an average 7.6% grade? Alpine Road runs from Pescadero Road (the 7.6-er, according to Grant Petersen's *Roads To Ride South*) up to the intersection of Skyline Drive (State Highway 35) and Page Mill Road. This 47-mile loop will take you up the killer, then back down to Pescadero on over 15 miles of sweeping descent.

Start at the corner of Stage and Pescadero Roads in Pescadero and ride east toward the mountains. Pescadero Road quickly turns north and runs through open farmland for almost seven miles before it starts to climb. Then the redwoods close in, and the going gets tougher, through the hamlet of Loma Mar and up past Memorial Park. Suddenly, the climb turns into a steep downhill for almost two miles, past Sam McDonald Park, ending at the Y that is the Alpine Road junction.

Here's where things get serious, folks. If you're already intimidated, you can bail out by turning left and riding out to State Highway 84. If not, turn right on Alpine. The next seven miles are nothing but up, most of it in the open and all of it a bear.

You'll be delighted to learn that, once you turn left on Skyline/Highway 35, it's mostly downhill for the next seven miles to Skylonda, at the intersection of Skyline and La Honda Road/Highway 84. This is a good place to stop for lunch, either take-out from the deli to your right, or sit-down at Alice's Restaurant on your left.

Make a left onto 84, and you'll descend again for over 14 miles to San Gregorio, where there's a General Store (hint: buy the bottled water; don't attempt to drink the brackish stuff out of their tap). Another left puts you on Stage Road for the seven mile up-and-down run back to Pescadero.

The Killer of Them All

Okay, okay, others may not agree with me. But everyone has his favorite killer to hate, and Redwood Gulch Road is mine. It's only a mile from Stevens Canyon Road up to Highway 9, but most of that mile is an 18% grade, and it was no place for me to be the very first time I rode with cleats. I fell over like the trike-riding chimp on "Laugh-In."

To keep the mileage down for this challenge, start at De Anza College in Cupertino, at the corner of Stelling and McClellan Roads and your distance will be little more than 15 miles total. Ride west on McClellan, down into the gulch that forms Stevens Creek and back up again to Foothill Road. Turn left and right, then left on Stevens Canyon Road.

You'll climb up past Stevens Canyon Reservoir, then descend into Stevens Creek County Park. At the Y, bear right to continue on Stevens Canyon as it begins to climb up into the redwoods. About a mile and a half up, you'll see a little red house on the left. The corner it sits on is the intersection with Redwood Gulch Road, which now has a sign and even appears on some maps (time was when it was the best-kept secret of commuters from the San Lorenzo Valley to Silicon Valley).

Don't forget to gear all the way down before you make the left turn onto Redwood Gulch. The grade on Stevens Canyon is already pretty steep (my guess would be about 6%), and it increases immediately at least 3%. In a quarter of a mile or so it doubles, and the rest of the climb stays just as bad, if not worse.

Just when you think you're going to die from this killer hill, Redwood Gulch peaks out and gives you a short downhill to Highway 9, more than halfway up toward Saratoga Gap. If you still want to climb, you can turn right and continue on up to the Gap at Highway 35.

This Pedal Tour, however, assumes you've had enough and turns left to descend Highway 9 toward Saratoga. Nevertheless, it does provide one more little ascent in order to avoid the Saratoga traffic. In about three and a half miles, turn left onto Pierce Road and climb the short grade up to the old Paul Masson Winery. Pass the winery for an almost two-mile downhill through new housing developments, old vineyards and horse ranches.

Just beyond the small vineyard on your left, look for a hidden left turn onto Comer Road. Take it, or you'll wind up on busy Saratoga-Sunnyvale Road. Make the next right onto Arroyo de Arguello and cruise down through the sumptuous Saratoga homes. Turn left on Via Roncole for one block to Prospect Road. A left on Prospect and a right on Stelling will bring you back to McClellan Road at De Anza College.

ROUTE SLIP

The Alpine Climb
From Pescadero Road and Stage Road in Pescadero

TURN	ON	FOR
East	Pescadero Road	11.5
Right	Alpine Road	7.5
Left	Skyline Drive/Highway 35	7.2
Left	La Honda Road/Highway 84	14.0
Left	Stage Road	7.3

Redwood Gulch
From De Anza College Tennis Courts, at Stelling & McClellan in Cupertino

TURN	ON	FOR
Left	McClellan Road	2.0
Left	Foothill Boulevard/Stevens Canyon Road	3.0
Bear right	At Y to stay on Stevens Canyon	1.5
Left	Redwood Gulch Road	0.75
Left	Highway 9	2.5

Left	Pierce Road	2.5
Left	Comer	0.1
Right	Arroyo de Arguello	0.75
Left	Via Roncole	0.1
Left	Prospect Road	0.25
Right	Stelling Road	1.1

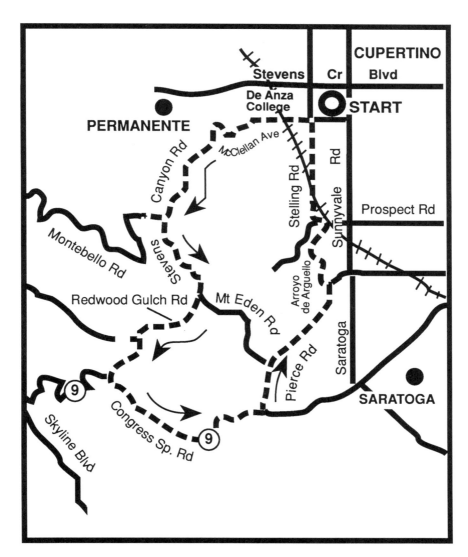

Top: Hills and levees of the East Bay as seen from the Visitor Center at San Francisco Bay Wildlife Refuge.

Left: There's more than one way to "wheel" around Ardenwood Farm.

3. EAST BAY
Solano, Contra Costa, Alameda, Yolo Counties

Ride the East Bay and you'll confront a fact of geography: almost all the riding is vertical! Before you know it, you're in the Berkeley Hills or the farther reaches of the Diablo Range. To share your suffering, sign up for the Grizzly Peak Century in early May. Or escape to the relatively rolling hills of Fremont and Newark. But look out for those steep Coyote Hills trails on your mountain bike!

Tilting at Windmills on Patterson Pass
April 1991

Ever drive over Altamont Pass on Interstate 580 between Livermore and Tracy and marvel at the hundreds of windmills on the hilltops? Did you know you could ride right up to some of those windmills?

There are seldom-traveled roads over both Altamont Pass and Patterson Pass. Altamont's such a surprisingly little bump, you barely even know you've climbed it, and the windmills are pretty much hidden from view. Patterson, on the other hand, is "a fun ride for fit bicyclists," says *Roads to Ride* author Grant Petersen, in what may have been the understatement of the '80s! It's a nice long uphill pull of six miles or so and at the top is haunted by windmills, high-frequency power lines and lots of empty space.

It's creepy! The electric fields crackle. The windmills are usually stopped, so even with the normally brisk breeze, they don't budge. And there's nothing else out there! When I made the ascent on the Cherry City Century last year, I topped out on the pass alone. My first instinct was to pedal as fast as my feet could go and get the hell off that hill! If I didn't, I was sure something was going to get me, and no one would ever know what happened!

This 43.5-mile route, which is loosely based on Cherry City's 100K and Bob deMille's Western Wheelers Long Distance Training Ride, starts at Carnegie Park in downtown Livermore and circles to climb both passes. Bob recommends two optional deviations: One is an alternate return for avid climbers who consider tiny Altamont beneath their abilities. The other's a short side trip to a California Aqueduct pumping station.

Both options take off from the turnaround point at Mountain House, a former stagecoach stop that is a motorcyclists' hangout at the junction of Grant Line, Midway and Altamont Pass roads. Mountain House is a good place to stop for lunch. They serve standard plastic microwave fare, but soda and beer are available, and there's a picnic area where you can eat your carry-along food.

For the tougher climb, take Grant Line Road to the Aqueduct Bike Trail, which parallels 580. After about six miles, exit onto Corral Hollow Road for a steady 10-mile climb followed by two miles of nontrivial grunt. On the way you'll pass an old mining town and an off-road motorcycle park, Carnegie Recreation Area, before descending six miles to Greenville Road on the east side of Lawrence Livermore Laboratories. Turn right to pick up the main route at Altamont Pass Road.

For an easier option, visit the Harvey Burns State Water Pumping Station, which pumps aqueduct water 245 feet up to the next level, and the park at Bethany Reservoir. The pumping station is about 100 yards up the hill on Mountain House Road, just beyond the intersection. A mile of riding to the top of the station brings you to the reservoir and park area, also a good place to eat your lunch.

No matter which direction you take, you'll encounter lots more bike-tilting inclines besides the ones holding windmills. Just gear down and keep pedalin'! Eventually you'll be back on the flats circling Livermore Labs through open rangeland before you encounter the downtown traffic. En garde!

ROUTE SLIP

From Carnegie Park, Third and J Streets in Livermore

TURN	ON	FOR
Right	South Livermore Avenue	1.1
Straight	Tesla	3.3
Left	Cross Road	2.2
Right	Patterson Pass Road	9.6
Left	Midway	2.9
	Mountain House on left at junction of Altamont Pass Road and Grant Line; Aqueduct Pumping Station on left about a quarter-mile beyond Mountain House	

Optional Alternate:

Right	Grant Line Road	
Right	Aqueduct Bike Path	6.0
	Dead flat, with tailwind!	
Right	Corral Hollow Road	18.0
	Becomes Tesla in Livermore	
Right	Greenville	2.1
	Pick up main route at Patterson Pass Road	

Or just turn:

Left	Altamont Pass Road	7.2
Left	Carroll	1.0
Straight	North Flynn	4.0

Right	Patterson Pass Road	1.2
Right	Greenville Road	1.8
Left	Northfront — *at Altamont Pass Road*	1.5
Right	Vasco Road	1.0
Left	Dalton	0.5
Right	Ames	0.2
Left	Raymond	1.0
Left	Lorraine St.	0.4
Right	Hartford	1.1
Left	North Livermore Avenue	3.5
Right	Third St. — to Carnegie Park	

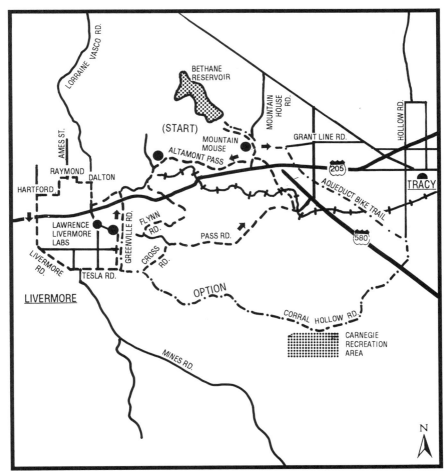

Ardenwood Farm

November 1986

Between the Dumbarton Bridge and Alameda Creek, down Fremont way, there's a farm that's not entirely a farm. Or maybe I should say it's an East Bay Regional Park that's something more than a park.

Ardenwood Historic Farm is a living history project of the type much publicized in Williamsburg, Virginia. Located on 205 acres of the original 6,000- acre Patterson Ranch in the open land sheltered from the Bay by the Coyote Hills, it recreates a self-sufficient 1880s working farm. For those of us who would rather pedal anywhere than drive, a visit to Ardenwood is a perfect excuse for a bike ride.

Kids love Ardenwood, and the park has many special programs for them. This 30-mile tour is easy enough for older kids with cycling experience to tackle, or for younger ones to ride comfortably in a trailer.

To reach Ardenwood Farm from the Peninsula, cross the Dumbarton Bridge and exit at Thornton Avenue. Turn left on Thornton and continue on Paseo Padre. At Newark Boulevard, turn left and cross under Highway 84, then turn right at the East Bay Parks sign into the park. The crossing is about 10 miles from Menlo Park, and a worthwhile addition to this tour.

From Union City BART, you can ride south on Decoto and pick up a bike path at the Highway 84 overpass just beyond 880 (the Nimitz Freeway, formerly State Highway 17). If the path is closed, continue on Decoto to Newark Boulevard. Turn right on Newark, then right again into Ardenwood.

First, Le Tour de Fremont

This route pretty much follows the 50-km option on the Fremont Freewheelers' Primavera Century. Former club president Lorraine Fletcher generously shared with me her maps and intimate knowledge of the area (she lives a scant mile from Ardenwood). She suggests starting early from the park so you can have plenty of time to explore when you return.

Begin your tour from the Ardenwood parking lot and ride back toward Ardenwood/Newark Boulevard. Turn right on Ardenwood and climb the freeway overpass. Look sharp for the entrance to the Alameda Creek Bike Trail on your right in about a mile and a half. Use caution riding through the gravel to enter the trail, which immediately gives way to pavement.

From here you have a few options. You can continue along Alameda Creek, enjoying the scenery and the birdwatching. Or you can exit in about 2.3 miles at the little unnamed park (complete with picnic tables, water and toilet) tucked in the "oxbow" of the creek where it turns east. If you'd prefer to stay on the trail, you can exit about 1.5 miles up at Isherwood. Or you can stick with it all the way out to Niles Canyon and pick up the route at Old Canyon Road.

If you exit at the park, ride out into the cul-de-sac at the end of Beard Drive. Make an immediate left on Whitehead, then another left on Paseo Padre Parkway (this road completely circles Fremont and Newark, so you will be using it repeatedly during this ride). In about a mile, you'll come to Isherwood, where you'll turn left, over the creek.

If you've followed the bike trail to Isherwood, it will be the second overpass you pass beneath. Exit on the far side of Isherwood, and you'll emerge on the right side of the street.

Isherwood becomes Quarry Lakes, a road you won't find on your AAA map. You'll pass colorful gladiola fields, part of the area's thriving flower seed industry. There's a real farm on the left, and Lorraine says to watch out for chickens crossing the road!

At the end of Quarry Lakes, turn right on Osprey, then right onto Alvarado-Niles Road. In about 1.5 miles, you'll approach downtown Niles. Avoid the traffic by ducking right on Hillview Drive, then left on Second Street and left on J Street. This brings you out to Niles Boulevard near the old railway car that serves as a chamber of commerce.

Turn right and follow Niles to the left under the overpass. Cross Mission and start up Niles Canyon Road. Then take the first right onto Old Canyon Road. Here is where the Alameda Creek bike trail finally ends. At the first opportunity, turn right on Clarke Drive and climb a tiny upgrade to Canyon Heights Drive. Turn right and follow Canyon Heights through a right/left jog at Maar Avenue to Morrison Canyon Road. Another right turn will bring you back out to Mission Boulevard.

Stay on Mission for 6.2 miles of gradual uphill with the prevailing wind at your back. At the top of the first long grade, you'll see the newly refurbished Mission San Jose on your left. A stop here offers a lesson in California history that goes back over a century more than the background of Ardenwood Farm.

Continuing on Mission, you'll ride up and down, passing Ohlone College and the entrance to Mission Peak Regional Preserve. Eventually, you'll encounter Paseo Padre again. Turn left here and climb up to a sweeping view of southern San Francisco Bay and a fast descent down East Warren Avenue. At Warm Springs Boulevard turn right and continue north as it first becomes Osgood (at Grimmer Boulevard) and then Driscoll (at Washington).

Finally, you'll turn left onto Paseo Padre one last time for a seven-mile ride past Fremont Central Park back north to Alameda Creek. The road doglegs left just before Northgate Park and crosses over Highway 880 on its way south. At Ardenwood, turn right and cross the Highway 84 overpass, and return to Ardenwood Farm on the left.

Meanwhile, Back at the Farm

Now you're ready for an afternoon of living history. You can ride straight from the old railway depot/ticket office on a horse-drawn train, or you can hop on a hay wagon for a tour around the park. On foot, you can take a tour of the main house, visit the granary, the blacksmith shop, the hay barn, the animal pens, and the horse corrals.

When I scouted this tour, I even met up with Ranger Frank Johns. Like other rangers and community volunteers at Ardenwood, he was dressed in period costume. But Frank could be easily distinguished from the rest when he was riding his "Bonecrusher" high-wheeler. If asked, he was usually happy to give riding lessons.

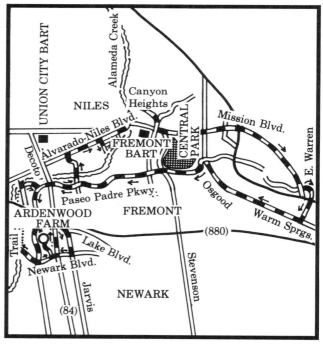

You can replace the calories you burned on your ride at the Chuck Wagon, where you can buy box lunches and fresh iced tea. Then work them off again by volunteering on one of the season's farming activities.

When I was there in October, they were harvesting hay with scythes and loading it on wagons with wooden pitch forks. Walnut harvesting with euca-lyptus poles was coming up in a couple of weeks. And a special Harvest Festival was planned for later in the month, featuring corn and pumpkin harvests, ice cream making, cider pressing, and square dancing.

Ardenwood Farm is open from April through November. Admission on weekends and holidays is $3 for adults and $2 for kids under 13; on Thursdays and Fridays it's $1.50 and $1 respectively. Bikes aren't allowed in the park, but you can lock them to the inward side of the chain link fence, within sight of folks in the ticket office.

For information on events planned for when you want to visit, call Ardenwood Historic Farm at 510-796-0663. If you can't make it in November, inquire about the special Christmas tours in December.

ROUTE SLIP

From Ardenwood Farm parking lot on Newark Boulevard in Newark

TURN	ON	FOR
Right	Ardenwood Boulevard	1.5
Right	Alameda Creek Recreational Trail	2.5
Right	Onto Beard Drive (cul-de-sac)	0.1
Immed. Left	Whitehead Lane	.75
Left	Paseo Padre Parkway	1.25
Left	Isherwood (over creek)	0.8
	Becomes Quarry Lakes	
Right	Osprey	
Right	Alvarado-Niles Road	1.5
Right	Hillview Drive	< 0.1
Left	Second Street	0.6
Left	J Street	< 0.1
Right	Niles Boulevard	0.4
	Turns left beneath underpass	
Continue	Old Canyon Road	0.2
Right	Old Canyon Road	0.8
Right	Clarke Drive	0.25
Right	Canyon Heights Drive	0.8
Right/Left	Maar Avenue	0.1
Right	Morrison Canyon Road	0.75
Right	Mission Boulevard	6.2
Left	Paseo Padre	0.6
Continue	East Warren Avenue	1.2
Right	Warm Springs Boulevard	4.5
	Becomes Osgood, then Driscoll	
Left	Paseo Padre	8.0
Right	Ardenwood Boulevard	1.0
Left	Ardenwood Farm	

Mountain Biking the East Bay Hills and Levees

August 1987

Some people have all the luck! When Lorraine and Richard Fletcher bought their home just across Alameda Creek from Fremont, they were both avid cyclists, but mountain biking was not part of their repertoire.

Today the Fletchers do most of their winter riding on mountain bikes, and quite a bit in the sunny seasons, too. In fact, they've become fat-tire addicts. But unlike the rest of us, they don't have to drive for miles before escaping the roar of internal combustion engines. They just jump on their mountain bikes and ride over the creek to Coyote Hills Regional Park and the San Francisco Bay National Wildlife Refuge.

For months, Lorraine and Rich had been regaling me with tales of steep climbs and thrilling descents in Coyote Hills, and of bird watching tours on the levees of the Wildlife Refuge. "Come on over and ride with us," they invited me. Who could resist?

We started right from their house and rode over to the Alameda Creek Regional Recreation Trail. This is actually two trails, one on the north side of the creek for equestrians, and one on the south side for hikers and cyclists. The trail runs for 12 miles, from the mouth of Niles Canyon on the south end of the creek to the Bay on the north end. It's a paved path that dives under bridges, then climbs back up again. And it's an ideal way to get to and from Coyote Hills, since it runs right along the northern end of the park.

If you drive across the Dumbarton Bridge to get to Coyote Hills, take Paseo Padre Parkway to Patterson Ranch Road, which ends at Park Headquarters, where you can pick up a map, fill your water bottle and make a pit stop.

When you look at the map, don't be fooled by the dotted line indicating "bicycle trail." That's a mere 3.5-mile paved bike path around the park, and although it will give you some nice views of the Bay, it's not exactly ideal mountain biking terrain. The off-road stuff is indicated on the map by smaller dotted lines. Specifically, the names are Red Hill Trail, Meadowlark Trail, and Cochenyo Trail. There are also a few links from the bike path to the trails, plus some hiking-only trails over boardwalks and through the marshes that are clearly marked with "No Bicycles" signs. But any trail without that sign is fair game.

According to Richard Fletcher, Fremont Freewheelers used to have a mountain bike ride every Monday evening that started out on the Cochenyo Trail, past the Indian Shell Mound, then out on one of the other trails. If you're exploring Coyote Hills, it's definitely worth a ride out

Cochenyo to see the mound. A shell mound, by the way, is an accumulation of shellfish remains tossed out by previous inhabitants, in this case the Ohlone Indians.

You can pick up the Red Hill Trail directly from the bike path where it connects with the Alameda Creek Trail on the northwest end of the park, then ride it all the way down to where the bike path loops around toward park headquarters. Or you can ride the Crossover Fire Trail west from the headquarters to the south end. Keep in mind that Red Hill is also an equestrian trail, where you can expect to encounter horses.

North of the Crossover Trail, Red Hill is a challenging up-and-down ride, with plenty of nontrivial climbs and descents. In fact, the first time I went down what Rich and Lorraine refer to as the "north hill" (obviously because it's north of all the others), I was so scared I yelled for my mama!

But the Fletchers don't recommend riding the section of Red Hill south of the crossover trail, even though there are rarely horses on it. That's because going downhill, "it's like dropping off a cliff," says Rich. As for tackling it in the other direction, "we've never gotten up it," he confesses.

South of the paved bike path, you have a choice of two trails. Meadowlark Trail takes you up Nike Hill, where you can detour on a paved driveway to the transmission tower and a view worth the climb. If you take Meadowlark all the way to the southern boundary of the park, you can loop back east of Nike Hill on a gravel trail that Rich says is "kind of steep in places."

Your other choice going south is to link up with the San Francisco Bay National Wildlife Refuge on the other side of the Highway 84 freeway. Just pick up the continuation of Red Hill Trail, which widens into a gravel road and skirts around a quarry to a pedestrian/bike bridge.

Although this bridge was built when the freeway was constructed, it remained officially closed to hikers and cyclists until this past April, when it emerged from the bureaucratic morass of interagency cooperation. Now that it's open, you can ride directly from Coyote Hills Regional Park to the National Wildlife Refuge Visitor Center by crossing the bridge and taking the short, paved climb on the other side.

Stop at the Visitor Center to check out the exhibits and pick up maps that show which levees are open for exploration. If you call well enough in advance and have a large enough group, you can even arrange for a docent to lead a cycling excursion around the refuge and describe the ecology of the mud flats, salt marshes and salt ponds. (Call 510-792-3178 for recorded information, 792-0222 to talk to a human being.)

If you're on your own, you may want to take a turn around the Tidelands Trail and read its numbered exhibits. Bikes are allowed, but you're requested to walk them down the dunes. On a clear day the view from the top of the dunes is magnificent and almost worth the hassle of

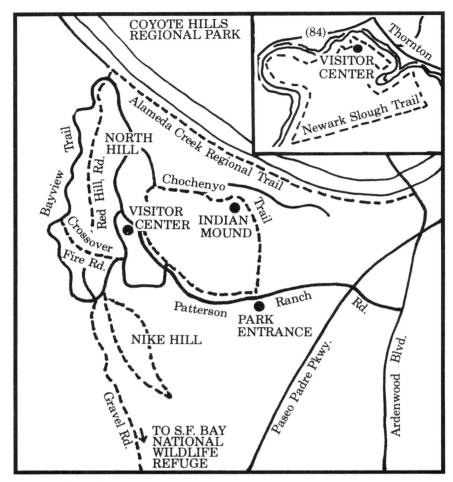

walking the bike.

The Tidelands Trail also gives you access to the Newark Slough Trail, a loop around the levees below the Visitor Center. Here's where you'll get to do plenty of bird watching. Just pedal along as quietly as you can and you won't disturb the birds at all. Then all you have to do is shift gears and you can watch them spread their wings and take off!

Riding around the slough trail can be a hair-raising experience; the headwinds are so stiff they can actually lift the hairs off your arms. Just gear down, tuck in and keep pedaling until you turn the corner and head back toward the Tidelands Trail with the wind at your tail.

You can return to Coyote Hills the way you came, over the pedestrian/

bike bridge. Or you can ride out to Thornton Avenue, cross the freeway and continue on Paseo Padre. Turn left onto Patterson Ranch Road, and you'll end up back at the park headquarters.

ROUTE SLIP

From Alameda Creek Trailhead on Ardenwood Boulevard

TURN	ON
Left	Alameda Creek Trail
Left	Red Hill Trail
Left	Crossover Fire Road
Right	Paved bike path to Nike Hill
Left	Nike Hill Loop/Meadowlark Trail
	Return to bike path
Right	Gravel trail to Wildlife Refuge
	Restrooms and info at Visitor Center
Continue	Tidelands Trail
Left or right	Newark Slough Trail

On-road return:

Left	Thornton Avenue
Continue	Paseo Padre Parkway
Left	Patterson Ranch Road to Coyote Hills Park Headquarters

Killer Hills East of San Francisco Bay

July 1985

In every cyclist's life there is at least one hill that feels more like a threat than a challenge. It may be only a squiggle on a map, but it's a pain in the knees when you're riding it.

This is what my office colleague Roland Dumas calls a "Killer Hill." His first killer was his own driveway, then progressed through a shallow climb to the Peninsula's Skyline Boulevard, then to the five-mile series of switchbacks featured on Kings Mountain Road. That's progress!

The point is that a Killer Hill is what you make it. And you can make it a lot less threatening by just getting out and riding the sucker until it no longer looms menacingly on the horizon.

These two Killer Hills are to be found east of San Francisco Bay, but they're not the only ones in the area. Consider, if you will, Wildcat Canyon, Grizzly Peak, Bear Creek and Castle Crest Roads (Altamont Pass, anyone?). If you're from the East Bay, you probably could name a lot more. But I'm sure you'll agree that Mt. Diablo is exhaustingly long, and Cantelowe Hill is pretty darned steep.

The Devil's Own Mountain

There are two approaches to Mt. Diablo, one from Walnut Creek on the north, and the other from Danville on the south. What I didn't realize when I rode the Devil Mountain Century is that the southern approach is actually easier than the northern one they chose. When Diane Harrison Utrecht used to lead her "BART to BART" ride from Fremont to Walnut Creek, she would tackle Diablo from the south.

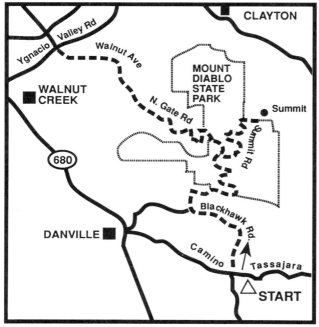

To pick up the last 30 miles of Diane's route, start at the corner of Camino Tassajara and Blackhawk Roads, about five miles east of Danville. Ride north on Blackhawk for 3.3 miles and turn right on Mt. Diablo Scenic Boulevard. In a mile the road changes to South Gate Road, six miles of climbing with an average grade of 4.5%.

At the ranger station, make a sharp right onto Summit Road and gear down some more for the 4.5 miles of oxygen deprivation to the top. The worst is the 17% grade for the last quarter mile or so. To reach the summit, take the narrow paved pathway leading to a view that Grant Petersen describes in *Roads to Ride* as "the second most panoramic in the world (Mt. Kilimanjaro is the first)."

This is probably a good place to talk about the Killer Hill climber's Number One Enemy — heat. During the summer, Mt. Diablo State Park has been known to shut down due to the fire hazards of hot, windy weather conditions. That gives you an idea of what this climb is like in the blazing sun of a mid-day in mid-July. Killer hills are best ridden in the early morning during the warmer seasons, and Mt. Diablo may well be the worst one to even consider this time of year.

You'll cool down on the descent, though. Start by retracing your tracks down Summit Road, then continue straight on North Gate Road. It's eight miles of downhill before you make a right at the sign for Oak Grove Road, followed by an immediate left onto Walnut Avenue to continue into Walnut Creek.

Note: *The original 1985 version of this first-ever Killer Hill ride did not provide a return route to Blackhawk. However, if you do love killers, you'll enjoy the 30 additional miles, including infamous Morgan Territory Road, on the route slip.*

The Surprise on Cantelowe Road

Bill Bryant describes Cantelowe Road as "flat with a moderately difficult climb, a neat little hill used many times on the Davis Fall Century.... It is guaranteed to get your attention." It sure got my attention when I found my-

self suddenly stoking a tandem up the 18% grade to the summit. *That* was the surprise!

This loop totals 22 miles, letting you warm up before and relax after the climb on Cantelowe. Start from the junction of Putah Creek and Winters roads, just south of the bridge into Winters, north of Davis. Ride west on Putah Creek for five miles to Pleasants Valley Road and turn left.

In about four miles, turn left on Cantelowe Road and shift down. According to Bill, "while the climb seemingly gets steeper with each revolution of your wheels, it is less than one mile in length." You could have fooled me! The summit offers a superior view of the Sacramento Valley, by the way.

Bill advises descending Cantelowe carefully, as it's a narrow country road that receives minimal attention from county maintenance crews. It winds through the Vaca Hills and ends in a short steep climb to Midway Road, where you make a right. A mile beyond Cantelowe there's a frontage road on the west side of Highway 505 that's not shown on many maps. The store here is used to catering to cyclists and is a good rest stop.

Continue north on the frontage road, which becomes Winters Road in two more miles (be sure to keep the freeway on your right). It's just five more flat miles to Putah Creek Road, and hard to believe you just did a killer hill.

ROUTE SLIPS

Mt. Diablo

From Camino Tassajara and Blackhawk Roads, east of Danville

TURN	ON	FOR
North	Blackhawk	3.3
Right	Mt. Diablo Scenic Boulevard	1.0
Continue	South Gate Road	6.0
Right	Summit Road at Ranger Station	4.5
	Take paved path to summit	
Reverse	Summit Road	4.5
Continue	North Gate Road	8.0
Right	Oak Grove Road	< 0.1
Immed. Left	Walnut Avenue to Ygnacio Valley Road	1.6

Return:

Not on map; adds 30 steep miles to route

Do not turn on Walnut Avenue; stay on Oak Grove		1.0
Right	Ygnacio Valley Road	4.0
Right	Clayton Road	1.5
Continue	Marsh Creek Road	4.5
Right	Morgan Territory Road	2.0
	Steep grades and sharp turns!	
Right	Highland Road	9.5
Right	Camino Tassajara to Blackhawk Road	5.2

Cantelowe Hill

From Putah Creek and Winters Roads, Winters

West	Putah Creek Road	5.0
Left	Pleasants Valley Road	4.0
Left	Cantelowe Road	5.0
Right	Midway Road	1.0
Left	Frontage Road at Highway 505	7.0
	Becomes Winters Road to Putah Creek Road	

4. SOUTH BAY
Santa Clara County

More climbs are in store when you head south to San Jose and the ranchlands beyond. But the pleasures outweigh the pain when you consider the rewards of the descents from the East San Jose hills, the ice cream in Los Gatos, or the wines of the Gilroy area. Or you can skip the hills altogether and discover a different kind of cycling adventure when you tackle urban San Jose on your mountain bike!

The Great Los Gatos Ice Cream Splurge!
June 1987

I know, I know. Ice cream is a nutritional no-no. I've read all those magazine articles, and I believe them. Too much fat. Too much sugar. Eat ice cream on a long, strenuous ride and you're just begging for the bonk.

Most of the time I go along with this sage advice and stick to the complex carbos that will get me through a long day's ride. But, "June is bustin' out all over," and something cool and soothing would sure hit the spot. Baskin-Robbins and Swenson's beckon from every corner. But I'm holding out until I get to Los Gatos. Because the ice cream there is so darned good, it's worth a spectacular splurge!

This 28-mile ride will take you from De Anza College in Cupertino to Los Gatos for at least one sample of the best ice cream south of the Golden Gate Bridge. You can reach De Anza by car from Highway 280 or Highway 85, where they intersect in Cupertino. Park at the college tennis courts, on McClellan just west of Stelling.

Mount up and ride out to McClellan. Turn left, then right onto Stelling and follow it as it curves left into Prospect. Make a right on Via Roncole for a block. At the end, turn right onto Ritanna, which becomes Arroyo de Arguello. At Wardell, turn left, cross Saratoga-Sunnyvale Road and continue on Cox.

Follow Cox all the way out to busy Quito Road, turn right and ride with the traffic for about a mile to Pollard. A left on Pollard will take you past the Rinconada Hills condos to Wedgewood Road. Take the right-turn lane onto Wedgewood, then turn left where Wedgewood intersects with Roxbury. You'll ride past La Rinconada Golf Club before turning right on Wimbledon, the lone street through the Courtside tennis and townhouse community.

At Winchester Boulevard, turn right, then jog immediately left onto Lark Avenue. Winchester's a heavily travelled access road to Los Gatos from San Jose and Campbell, and there's a double left-turn lane here, the right half of which is also a through lane. So use a heavy dose of caution when you "jog."

From Lark, make an immediate left onto University Avenue and ride for over two miles through Los Gatos' mini-extension of Silicon Valley's high-tech industry, past Vasona Park, and across Highway 9.

If you're an old-fashioned hand-made ice cream nut, you may want to make a right turn onto Bachman, then a left onto Santa Cruz Avenue to sample the fare at Bay Area-renowned Double Rainbow. But if it's gelato that turns you on, stick with me, kid. The *crème de la crème* is yet to come.

At the end of University, make a left turn on Main Street and cross the bridge over the Highway 17 freeway. About another block further, look on your left for Dolce Spazio (it means "sweet spot"). You can stop here and cut the round trip to 20 moderate miles by skipping the climb. But if you really want to earn your splurge, keep going for a couple of good, stiff uphills before pigging out.

Continue on up the short hill at the end of Main Street, which then becomes Los Gatos Boulevard. At Kennedy Road, turn right and prepare to climb. It's easy going at first, including a couple of surprising downgrades, before the really hard work starts. Look for the sign at Top of the Hill Road on your right; when you reach it, you've reached the summit.

The descent is rapid and full of switchbacks, ending at the stop sign at Shannon Road. Stay alert and be prepared to gear down quickly as you turn left into Shannon's steep uphill grade. If you flub it, turn right on Shannon and ride out a ways on the flat before you turn around for an easier downshift.

The one-mile climb on Shannon is narrow and twisty, and you may have to deal with fast-moving motor traffic. The summit is just beyond the driveway into the horse-breeding ranch on your right. Then it's a mile and a half of sweet, easy-to-negotiate downhill back to town.

To avoid riding on congested Los Gatos Boulevard again, turn left off Shannon onto Englewood (one block beyond the bike route sign), then right on Kennedy. Cross Los Gatos Boulevard at the light and continue on Caldwell to Bella Vista. Turn left and take in the view of Los Gatos Canyon before you charge downhill to the stop sign at Pleasant Avenue. Make a left, then a right onto Main Street.

Now it's time for that splurge! Roll on up to Dolce Spazio and order one of their special one-of-a-kind flavors. Try Kahlua, Oreogasmic, or Almond Amaretto (my favorite). This block was devastated by the Loma Prieta Earthquake in October 1989, but Dolce Spazio, along with many of its neighbors, is back on the scene.

Main Street is the Los Gatos version of bikie heaven. You'll spot bicycles of every description, in every direction. Once, there was even an old-timer bouncing along Main Street on a classic Schwinn Panther, complete with

Gearin' up for gellato in Los Gatos, before the quake of '89.

a springer fork for front-wheel suspension! These days the social center is the Los Gatos Coffee Roasting Company, opposite the University Avenue intersection with Main Street. There are also several small restaurants where you can sit inside and still keep an eye on your bike.

Replete with butterfat, glucose and exotic flavors, you can now turn around and retrace your tracks. Better still, explore a few more new roads on this slightly different return route, which features a few short climbs to help you work off the extra calories.

Return on Main Street to University and ride past Highway 9 to Blossom Hill Road. Turn left at the light, then jog right at the next light onto Santa Cruz Avenue. In about a quarter of a mile, turn left onto Daves (look for a bike route sign). Daves climbs a bit, then makes a couple of sharp turns and climbs again. Just before the top, turn right onto Via Caballero, which becomes Twin Creeks at the bottom of the hill.

Twin Creeks brings you out to Quito Road, where a jog left will take you to Sobey Road. Turn right and climb a little again, then head downhill for about a mile. (Try not to gawk too much at the sumptuous homes in this neighborhood!) Make a left onto Ten Acres for some more up-and-down, then a right on Chester for the last downhill.

At Allendale, turn left, ride past West Valley College and make a right on Fruitvale. Cross Saratoga Avenue by turning right, then immediately

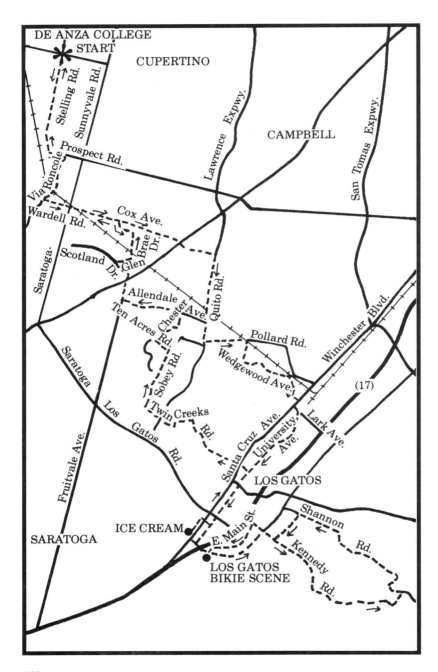

DE ANZA COLLEGE
START
CUPERTINO

Stelling Rd.
Sunnyvale Rd.

CAMPBELL

Lawrence Expwy.
San Tomas Expwy.

Prospect Rd.

Via Roncole

Wardell Rd.
Cox Ave.

Saratoga-
Scotland Dr.
Glen
Brae Dr.

Allendale Ave.
Chester Ave.
Quito Rd.

Ten Acres Rd.
Sobey Rd.
Pollard Rd.

Wedgewood Ave.
Winchester Blvd.

Twin Creeks Rd.
(17)

Saratoga
Los Gatos Rd.
Santa Cruz Ave.
University Ave.
Lark Ave.

Fruitvale Ave.
LOS GATOS

Shannon

ICE CREAM
Kennedy Rd.

SARATOGA
E. Main St.

LOS GATOS
BIKIE SCENE

Rd.

and cautiously left onto Scotland. At Glen Brae, turn right and ride down to Cox.

From here on, you're reversing your route out: Cross Saratoga-Sunnyvale and continue on Wardell, then turn right on Arroyo de Arguello, left on Via Roncole, left on Prospect and right on Stelling. At McClellan turn left, then right into the De Anza parking lot.

Now that you've had a taste of Los Gatos' finest, I'm sure you'll be eager to return. For variety, try riding over Shannon or Kennedy from Almaden Valley, or make your connection via Los Gatos-Almaden Road.

If you're on the other side of the hill in Santa Cruz, ride up Old San Jose Road from Soquel to Summit, then drop down to Lexington Reservoir via Old Santa Cruz Highway. Ride around the reservoir and walk down the face of the dam to Los Gatos Creek Trail, which terminates at the Main Street bridge over Highway 17, just across the street from Dolce Spazio.

ROUTE SLIP

From De Anza College Tennis Courts, McClellan Road off Stelling in Cupertino

TURN	ON	FOR
Left	McClellan Road	0.1
Right	Stelling Road	1.6
Left	Prospect Road	0.25
Right	Via Roncole	0.1
Right	Ritanna	0.60
	Becomes Arroyo de Arguello	
Left	Wardell Road	0.3
Continue	Cox Avenue	2.25
Right	Quito Road	1.25
Left	Pollard Road	0.6
Right	Wedgewood	0.25
Left	Wedgewood at Roxbury	0.75
Right	Wimbledon	0.4
Right	Winchester	0.1
Immed. Left	Lark Avenue	0.1
	Use right left-turn lane	
Immed. Right	University Avenue	2.5
Left	Main Street	1.0
	Becomes Los Gatos Boulevard	
Right	Kennedy Road	3.25
	2.25 miles to summit	
Left	Shannon Road	2.5
	Sharp uphill turn!	
	1.2 miles to summit	

Left	Englewood	0.5
	Follow Bike Route signs	
Right	Kennedy	0.25
	Cross Los Gatos Boulevard	
Continue	Caldwell Avenue	0.15
Left	Bella Vista	0.5
Left	Pleasant Avenue	0.15
Right	Main	0.25
	Dolce Spazio on right	

Return:

Right	Main	0.2
Right	University	1.0
Left	Blossom Hill Road	0.1
Immed. Right	Santa Cruz Avenue	0.25
Left	Daves	0.75
	Follow bike route signs	
Right	Via Caballero	0.75
	Becomes Twin Creeks	
Left	Quito	0.1
Immed. Right	Sobey Road	1.0
Left	Ten Acres Road	0.3
Right	Chester Avenue	0.5
Left	Allendale Avenue	0.75
Right	Fruitvale Avenue	0.25
Right	Saratoga Avenue	0.1
Immed. Left	Scotland Drive	0.25
	Turn with caution!	
Right	Glen Brae Drive	0.75
Left	Cox	0.75
Continue	Wardell	0.3
Right	Arroyo de Arguello	0.6
Left	Via Roncole	0.1
Left	Prospect	0.2
Right	Stelling	1.6
Left	McClellan	0.1
	To De Anza tennis courts	

Fat-Tired Urban Assault: San Jose's Other Side

February 1985

Who would have thunk it? The ideal bike for handling city traffic, city potholes and city distances turns out to be a mountain bike! With two sets of tires, you can have a fleet of bicycles. Use your knobbies and you're ready for the dirt. Use your street tires and you're ready for almost anything.

Now, just suppose you could have your cake and eat it too. Just once, wouldn't you like to keep the knobbies on in town and have them do more than impersonate a semi?

Bern Smith came up with this idea for bringing dirt riding into the urban environment when he was living and working in San Jose. He started by riding his mountain bike to his job at Phil Wood & Co., then he joined some buddies to explore out-of-the-way routes around town. They discovered that creek and river levees, railroad beds and back alleys offer plenty of excitement and challenge for dirt riding and rock hopping, if you're willing to put up with a little "off-dirt" riding (that's pavement to you roadies) to make connections.

There are actually two versions of Bern's original Urban Assault. One travels south on Coyote Creek to Hellyer Park, where you can return to childhood by challenging the BMX course next to the Velodrome. The route described here, however, is somewhat shorter (around nine miles) and turns north on Coyote Creek, returning via the Guadalupe River. It offers a unique opportunity to acquire a special off-road skill — jumping converging railroad tracks from gravel bed to gravel bed! And if you've never forded a stream before, you'll get to try it on this one.

Unfortunately, there are a few aspects to seeing San Jose "inside out," as Bern puts it, that are not what you'd prefer for a mountain bike ride. It's hardly a wilderness experience. For instance, you'll learn how noisy an airport can really be, and you'll pass by the homeless who camp out along the rivers and under the bridges. Just the view of the weapons storage yard at FMC, Bern claims, can inspire you to "plot escape paths along the way for when the revolution comes."

Still, there are some pleasant surprises in store. For instance, the first time I rode with Bern on this route, the weeds along Coyote Creek were bursting with milky-white seedpods. They had already blanketed the trail and the slight breeze of our passing brought more out into the air. It was like riding on an inch or two of fresh snow, but the "snow" adhered to the mud on our tires. Soon we looked like we'd been tarred, feathered and run out of town!

Start your Urban Assault from the San Jose Round House at the Southern Pacific Freight Yard on Lenzen Avenue near Stockton. The easiest way to drive there would be to take Highway 880 to Coleman to Taylor to Stockton.

Ride east on Lenzen to the end and turn right onto the railroad right-of-way. Then it's welcome to Gravel City! Follow the tracks behind the FMC tank factory at First Street. You'll need to start practicing your jumping skills right away as the tracks begin to merge. Keep riding north as you cross the numbered downtown streets, up through Tenth. Take the tracks over the bridge at U.S. 101, past Old Bayshore and Schallenberger.

As soon as you cross the bridge over Coyote Creek, turn left onto the levee and follow the creek under Highway 880 and Montague Expressway. The trail will end about a mile past Montague, where you'll have to ford the stream and find the levee trail on the west side.

Turn north again and continue all the way up to Alviso-Milpitas Road/ Highway 237. Make a left here to head west toward the bridge over the Guadalupe River. If you have the time and the inclination, you can keep going past the bridge, turn right on Gold Street, ride into Alviso and seek out the short levee trail system into the San Francisco Bay National Wildlife Refuge. The birdwatching out there is often superior.

Meanwhile, back at the Guadalupe, the river has rideable levees on both sides, so take the one you prefer for your return south. You'll pass the Fairway Glen Golf Course and part of Agnews State Hospital, which sits on the former James Lick property (now developed in true Silicon Valley style). Then pass under Montague Expressway again, Trimble Road and 101 to the Municipal Airport. After pedaling the length of the airport, it's under Highway 880 to Taylor Street.

At Taylor, go two blocks west to Vendome, make a left and ride to Coleman to pick up the river trail again. The levee will cross the railroad tracks behind the FMC plant, where you started out. Just turn right onto the tracks to return to the Round House at Lenzen.

ROUTE SLIP

Please keep in mind that, like all mountain bike rides, this one offers ample opportunity to strike out in all directions, and to get lost without ever attempting to do so. Mileages, under the circumstances, are pretty much useless, and so are omitted here.

From the Southern Pacific Freight Yard, Lenzen Avenue east of Stockton, in San Jose

TURN	ON
East	Lenzen
Right	Railroad right of way
	Cross U.S. 101, Old Bayshore, Schallenberger,
	Coyote Creek
Left	Coyote Creek levee
	Ford creek approx. 1 mile beyond Montague Expressway
Left	Highway 237

Optional Side Trip:

Continue	237 to Gold Street
Right	Gold Street
Left	Elizabeth

Right	Hope
	Pick up levee trail system near marina parking lot
Left	Guadalupe River levee
	Cross beneath Montague, Trimble Road, U.S. 101
	Continue through airport, under Highway 880
Left	Taylor Street
Left	Vendome
Right	At Coleman, onto levee again
Right	Railroad tracks at FMC plant
Right	At Round House on Lenzen

Mission Trails Wine Tour
July 1983

This ride originally appeared in a column of five pedal tours, back in the days when I thought I'd never run out of roads to ride.

No need to travel to Napa Valley to take a wine tasting tour. Some of the most interesting wineries in central California are located around Morgan Hill and Gilroy, and the territory makes for a fine 22-mile bike tour. The route described here features three wineries; you may want to add a few, or cut back, depending on your ability to handle both alcohol and pedaling.

The easiest place to start is at the Mission Trails Delicatessen on Monterey Street in Morgan Hill. There's a convenient parking lot in the rear, and you can also buy your lunch to eat at a winery later.

First stop: Sycamore Creek Winery (reservations suggested). Take Monterey south to Dunne Avenue, turn right, then left on Dewitt, right on Edmondson, left on Oak Glen and right on Sycamore for a quick, steep climb. At Watsonville Road, turn right, then right again on Uvas and left into Sycamore Creek Winery.

After tasting, go back out to Watsonville Road and turn right, then left into Kirigin Winery. The route continues on Watsonville Road to Hecker Pass Highway (152), where you turn right, then right into Fortino Winery. This is the best place for lunch. Not only are there picnic tables, Fortino also runs a small deli behind the winery. Be sure to check out the unique T-shirts as well as the jug reds, among the best in the area.

After lunch, you can turn right on Highway 152 and ride beyond Fortino towards the pass to drop in at Hecker Pass Winery. Or turn left and visit Thomas Kruse and/or Summerhill Vineyards on your way toward Gilroy and the route home.

Be prepared for strong headwinds when you turn left from Highway 152 at Santa Teresa onto Morey. After Morey becomes Murphy, turn left on Fitzgerald, then right on Turlock, right on Highland, and left on

Coolidge. Coolidge will bring you onto Santa Teresa for a nontrivial but short climb onto Sunnyside. Turn right on Edmondson and retrace your tracks back to Monterey Street.

If you'd rather avoid the left turn onto Monterey, cross it and continue to a left on Depot Street, then left on Second Street, crossing Monterey again to the Mission Trails Deli.

A word of caution: It's fun to joke about drinking and riding, but it's not so funny if an accident occurs. Mixing wine tasting and cycling can be dangerous. One suggestion might be to convince a friend to drive a sag wagon along, both to pick up overindulgers and to carry the wines you purchase!

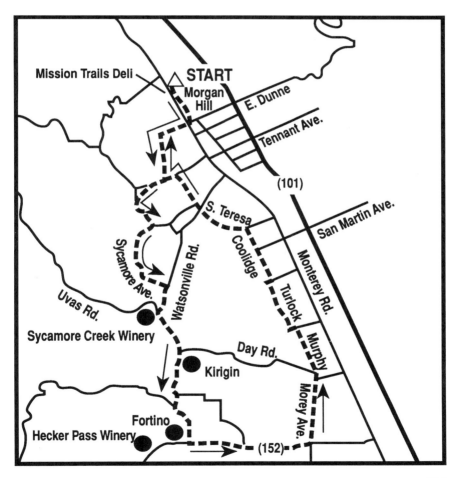

ROUTE SLIP

Mission Trails Deli on Monterey Highway in Morgan Hill

TURN	ON	FOR
Left	Monterey Highway	0.5
Right	Dunne Avenue	0.75
Left	Dewitt Avenue	1.0
Right	Edmondson Avenue	0.5
Left	Oak Glen Avenue	1.0
Right	Sycamore Avenue	0.75
Right	Watsonville Road	0.25
Left	Uvas Road	0.1
Immed. Left	Sycamore Creek Winery	
	Reservations suggested	
Right	Uvas	0.1
Right	Watsonville	1.2
Left	Kirigin Winery	
Right	Watsonville	2.4
Right	Hecker Pass Highway (152)	0.1
Immed. Right	Fortino Winery	
	To visit Hecker Pass Winery, turn right	
	For Thomas Kruse & Summerhill Vineyards, turn left	
Left	Hecker Pass/Highway 152	3.0
Left	Morey	1.5
	At Santa Teresa	
Continue	Murphy	0.5
Left	Fitzgerald	0.1
Right	Turlock	1.0
Right	Highland	0.1
Left	Coolidge	2.0
	Becomes Santa Teresa	
Continue	Sunnyside	1.0
Right	Edmondson	2.0
Left	Monterey	1.4
	To Mission Trails Deli	

South Bay Killer Hills
February 1986

Go north, east or west of San Francisco Bay, and you're bound to find a hill climb that takes the most out of you. But pedal on down San Jose way, and you'll find more than one. More than two. Would you believe more than six (if you don't count the off-road stuff)?

The South Bay is the place for riding killer hills. I'm not talking about Mt. Hamilton; that's got to be the easiest climb (and one of the longest) in the entire West. The climbs I'm referring to are more like Hamilton's side roads — Quimby, Clayton, and that early surprise on the Mt. Hamilton Challenge known as Crothers.

Two readers made sure I knew about almost every opportunity for pain and suffering south of the Bay. Larry Ames of San Jose reminded me about the loop around Almaden-Quicksilver Park on Hicks Road. Perry Stout, who left the South Bay hills for the Central Valley flats, recommended the two highest mountains in the district — Loma Prieta and Mt. Umunhum — for dirt riders (neither has paved roads near the top).

But both agreed that Sierra Grade deserves "top honors" in the killer hill category. You're right, guys; I'd already nominated it for this book. But I'm disappointed that neither of you mentioned my second choice, Metcalf Road. It may be relatively short, but it still meets my killer criteria: a hill that represents more threat than challenge when it appears on the horizon. It could be an extended climb of several miles or only two blocks long and virtually vertical. What really makes it a killer is how far you're willing to go to avoid climbing it, compounded by how much bragging you do when you finally conquer the sucker. Subjective, maybe, but it works!

One word of caution, however. South Bay killer hills are nearly all exposed to the ravages of sun and wind. Late fall, winter and early spring are the best times to tackle them. Summer is a definite no-no, unless you ride early in the morning and take along plenty of water and sunscreen.

San Jose's Own Sierra

You probably thought you'd have to head for the Sierras if you wanted to do 2,000 feet of climbing in less than four miles. But all you have to do is ride to east San Jose and head over the hill to Milpitas — the long way!

This 17-mile loop starts from Penitencia Creek Park, off Capitol Avenue on Penitencia Creek Road. Ride east on Penitencia Creek toward Alum Rock Park for about three-quarters of a mile and make a left on Piedmont. It's another three-quarters of a mile to a right on Sierra Road. Sorry, folks, that's just about all the warm-up you'll get!

Perry claims the steepest part of the climb is a 12% grade, while Grant Petersen puts it at 10% in *Roads to Ride South*. Regardless, it's a real haul for the first two miles, and the next two don't let up all that much, either. There's next to nothing to catch your interest at the top, except your breath. The next mile and a half are rolling, until the road becomes Felter Road and heads downhill.

That downhill is another four miles of thrills and chills. Said Perry, "I have tucked on the long straight-away descent and have hit over 55 miles an hour!" I believe him. Although the retrograde is almost nil, so is the traffic. The only company you'll have are your riding companions and a few cows.

You'll hardly notice when the road changes again to Calaveras Road, which drops down from the reservoir to the north. You'll continue sailing down through Ed Levin Park (restrooms) into Milpitas. Make a left on Piedmont, which becomes Old Piedmont in a little over a mile, then returns to Piedmont just before you cross Sierra Road again on your way back to Penintencia Creek Park.

Metcalf Road

Metcalf Road is probably the shortest killer hill on my list, but it still offers plenty of challenge, some 35 miles of beautiful countryside, and some pretty unusual scenery.

If you start from Santa Teresa Park at the end of Bernal Road south of Santa Teresa Boulevard, you'll have plenty of time to warm up before the climb. Ride north on Bernal for about a mile and exit onto Monterey Road South. In order to do this, you have to make a left from the freeway overpass, requiring an extra measure of caution. (Monterey Road is the former "Blood Alley," now nearly devoid of traffic thanks to the new U.S. 101 freeway.)

In 1.3 miles turn left onto Metcalf Road and cross U.S. 101. Once over the freeway, you'll gradually begin climbing for about two miles of 10.7% grade. This is the killer. At the top, relax and watch the antics of the dirt motorbikers at the County Motorcycle Park. Don't worry, they'll be staring at you, too.

The rest of the ride is gentle in comparison. According to Grant Petersen, there's a great blue heron's pond on the downhill that's easy to miss, and the UTC chemical plant, which isn't. The last mile and a half is uphill again, ending at San Felipe Road.

Turn left and ride the 6.5 rolling miles to Yerba Buena, which will connect you to what's left of Silver Creek Road, once the most idyllic of country roads and now given over to private development, and closed to public traffic. If you're looking for a neat place to have lunch, turn right on Aborn and ride up to Mirassou Winery. To continue on the loop, turn back onto San Felipe before the winery. From here it's nine miles back to Metcalf and a retrace of your tracks to Santa Teresa Park.

ROUTE SLIP

Sierra Grade

From Penitencia Creek Road and Capitol Avenue in San Jose

TURN	ON	FOR
Left	Penitencia Creek Road	0.75
Left	Piedmont Road	0.75
Right	Sierra Road	5.5
Continue	Felter Road	4.5
Continue	Calaveras Road	2.0
	Restrooms at Ed Levin County Park on left	
Left	Piedmont	4.0
	To Penitencia Creek Park	

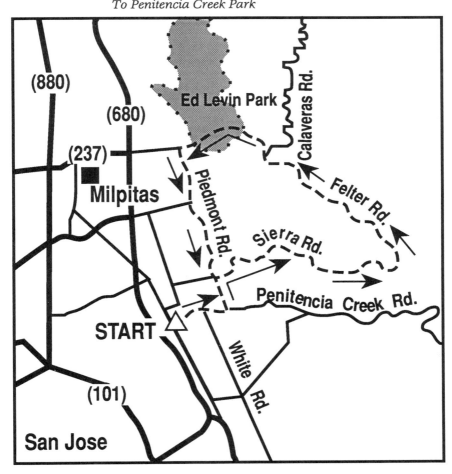

Metcalf Road

From Santa Teresa Park, end of Bernal Road, San Jose

TURN	ON	FOR
North	Bernal	2.0
Right	Monterey Road	1.3
	Cross U.S. 101 and exit onto Monterey Road	
Left	Metcalf Road	5.5
Left	San Felipe Road	6.5
Left	Yerba Buena	2.0
Right	Silver Creek	1.0
Right	Aborn Road	2.2
Right	San Felipe	9.0
Right	Metcalf	5.5
Right	Monterey	0.3
Left	Bernal — *to Santa Teresa Park*	2.0

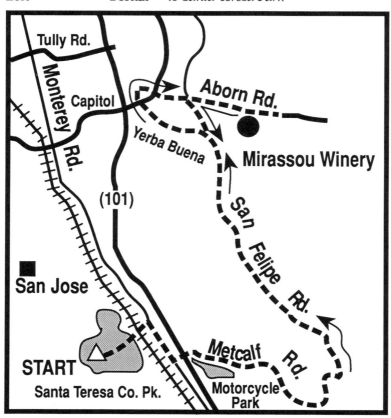

5. MONTEREY BAY AREA
Santa Cruz, San Benito, Monterey Counties

Go south toward "the other Bay" and you'll discover new rides that are the stuff of legends in California: redwoods, beaches, surf, fog and sunshine (both liquid and otherwise). Many of the roads — like Mountain Charlie and Jamison Creek — are steep beyond belief. But more of them — such as Lodge Road and the dirt trails at Wilder Ranch — are just as unbelievably scenic. All contribute to the local color of the Monterey Bay Area...with enough tradition, romance and history to satisfy any pedal tourist.

Mountain Charlie Rides Again
June 1985

The good news about this ride is that in 33.5 miles it offers some 28 miles of pure pleasure — zippy downhills, flatlands, or easy-to-moderate climbing. The bad news is the last five miles of uninterrupted vertical known as Mountain Charlie Road.

Bob Wall, who invented this tour from the Santa Cruz Mountains summit to Capitola and back, is known as a fellow with a sense of humor. But it's no joke when you hit the steep grades on Mountain Charlie, although they do have some attractions. The scenery can actually be breathtaking. And if you've ever ridden with Bob on this excursion, you probably learned to make the pain a little more bearable while thinking up ways to get even with him.

The ride begins from the improvised "Park and Ride" road shoulder on Summit Road just east of the Highway 17 overpass. Start as if you were going to ride east on Summit, but instead make a left onto Mountain Charlie Road for almost a mile of downhill to Old Santa Cruz Highway. Then turn right and ride the short distance back up to Summit.

Turn left and continue to Old Soquel-San Jose Road for the 13-mile downhill to Monterey Bay. The road name changes to Porter Street in Soquel, then to Bay Street after you pass under Highway 1 into Capitola.

At Capitola Avenue, turn right and ride down into the downtown area. Here you can buy a deli lunch and eat it on the beach or hit any of the good sit-down restaurants along the Esplanade. Wherever you choose to eat, make sure you carboload for the upcoming climb.

After refueling, return to Capitola Avenue and turn on Stockton to cross the bridge over Soquel Creek. Weather permitting, you'll enjoy a great view of Capitola Bay as you bear left and climb up Portola Road.

At the Y in the road turn left on Opal Cliff Drive and continue to 41st

Avenue, where you'll make another left, followed by an immediate right onto Cliff Drive. After riding about 3.5 miles along the beach and passing through the surfing community at Pleasant Point, follow East Cliff to the right and left at Seventeenth Avenue. Continue on to Twin Lakes Beach, where you'll make a right on Seventh Avenue, away from the shore.

Ride up to Eaton and turn left to cross the bridge at the Santa Cruz Yacht Harbor. Continue on Murray on the other side, turn right over a small bridge and pick up East Cliff again for a short downhill to the mouth of the San Lorenzo River and a view of the Santa Cruz Beach and Boardwalk.

At Ocean Avenue turn right and ride up to the busy Water Street intersection. Make a right at the light, then a left onto Market Street at Adolph's Restaurant. Market becomes Branciforte Drive at the beginning of your climb back up to the summit.

In about 1.6 miles you'll come to Glen Canyon Road, where you'll turn left for one of the easiest climbs you'll ever find. It was quite an experience to see my speedometer read more than 20 mph going uphill! (Must have been a tailwind.)

It's about 3.75 miles to Mount Hermon Road. Here you make a right, then another right on Scotts Valley Road, and an immediate left onto Bean Creek Road for another three miles of moderate climbing.

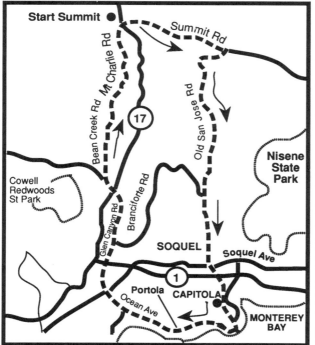

Turn left at Glenwood and follow the ridge. Watch for the heavier traffic and for Mountain Charlie Road on the left. It comes up suddenly and is easy to miss if you're not looking sharp!

Mountain Charlie starts out plenty easy, but don't be fooled by the shallow grades. The going gets pretty tough in just a mile or so. But as the going gets tougher, the scenery gets more interesting. You'll top a difficult grade, round a switchback and suddenly be facing a broad canyon, its sides thick with redwoods and oaks and dotted with houses.

You'll know you're approaching Summit when you see the signs for Riva Ridge and the climbing becomes easier again. Turn right when you reach the intersection and cross Highway 17 to return to the starting point. The nicest surprise is that you get to do this part downhill, and the overpass is blessedly flat.

ROUTE SLIP

From Summit Road just east of Highway 17

TURN	ON	FOR
Left	Summit Road	< 0.1
Immed. Left	Mountain Charlie Road	1.0
Right	Old Santa Cruz Highway	0.25
Left	Summit Road	2.0
Right	Old Soquel-San Jose Road	11.0
Continue	Porter Street	0.4
Continue	Bay Street	0.8
Right	Capitola Avenue	1.0
Right	Stockton over bridge	< 0.1
Bear left	Portola Drive	0.5
Left	Opal Cliff Drive	0.8
Left	41st Avenue	< 0.1
Immed. Right	East Cliff Drive	2.5
Left	East Cliff Drive at 17th Avenue	0.8
	Cheese Factory on the right	
Right	7th Avenue	0.75
Left	Eaton	1.0
Continue	Murray	0.7
Right	East Cliff Drive	0.5
Right	Ocean Street	1.0
Right	Water Street	0.75
Left	Market Street	1.0
Continue	Branciforte Drive	1.6
Left	Glen Canyon Road	3.75
Right	Mt. Hermon Road	0.5
Right	Scotts Valley Drive	0.2
Left	Bean Creek Road	3.0
Left	Glenwood Drive	1.0
Left	Mountain Charlie Road	4.0
Right	Summit Road and over Highway 17	0.25

Big Basin State Park

June 1988

It must be at least five years now since the last official Big Basin Mini-Challenge rolled through the hills surrounding Highway 9 and the San Lorenzo River. Sponsored by the Santa Clara Valley Bicycle Association, the Mini-Challenge offered three options starting from Big Basin State Park headquarters.

The 25-mile loop took riders out to Highway 9 via Highway 236, down Highway 9 to Boulder Creek and back to the park on Highway 236/Big Basin Way. The 50-mile and 100-km courses went on to Ben Lomond and Felton, with plenty of challenging climbs and dizzy descents en route.

This ride retraces most of the 50-mile Mini-Challenge, with an option to take the extra loop on the 100K. The total mileages here are actually a bit shorter, 44 miles and 56 miles respectively. But the biggest differences are a couple of delightful new twists added by Skyline Cycling Club ride leader Mimi St. Clair. The first takes you on a delightful detour from Ben Lomond to East Zayante. The second brings you back to Big Basin on a little-known side road unrivaled for scenic beauty.

To reach the traditional starting point, take Highway 9 from Saratoga, or from Highway 35 (Skyline Boulevard), south toward Santa Cruz. Bear right onto Highway 236 and drive directly to Park Headquarters. From Santa Cruz, drive north on Highway 9 to Boulder Creek and turn left onto Highway 236 (Big Basin Way) to reach Park Headquarters. With the latest rate hike (1991), parking is $6.00 per car, but it still gets pretty crowded on nice days, so try to get there early. You'll find a snack bar and restrooms right across the street from the parking lot.

Also, be warned that you will have no access to food and water the first 20 miles of the ride. So stock up at home, at Big Basin (limited choices), or in Felton, the last outpost of retail civilization.

The first 10 miles of your ride will be a good warmup for the challenge to come; it's a short, moderate upgrade, followed by a long downgrade on Highway 236 into Boulder Creek. Turn right at Highway 9 and continue on to Ben Lomond. Take extra care on this busy road; the traffic can be heavy and there's often no shoulder. If you're like me, you'll be glad to get the 3.75 miles over with.

Once in Ben Lomond, look for a bike route sign pointing to the left just beyond the fire station and follow it onto Glen Arbor Road. About a mile down Glen Arbor, look for Quail Hollow Road on the left (you'll see a sign for Loch Lomond Reservoir). Quail Hollow actually merges here with Glen Arbor; once you make the turn, you'll "double back" in the direction you came. Even though it feels like you're returning to Ben Lomond, you'll soon switch back in the right direction. Quail Hollow brings you into a stiff

Zayante Fire Station at the corner of Quail Hollow and East Zayante.

climb ending in a nice view and a very fast drop into the remote settlement of Zayante.

Cross Zayante Creek at the end of Quail Hollow, turn right on East Zayante Road and ride another two miles to Graham Hill Road. Turn right and in about half a mile you'll be at the main intersection in downtown Felton. Here's your last chance for food and water. But you may not want to eat heavily — you're about to embark on the toughest climb of the ride.

Directly across Highway 9 from Graham Hill Road, you'll start up Felton-Empire Road, a 3.7-mile, average 8% grade through Fall Creek and Henry Cowell State Parks to Empire Grade. Don't let that 8% average fool you — you'll tackle about a quarter of a mile of 14% within the first two miles! The road is smooth, though, and the shade is a blessing on a hot day.

At the top, you'll be faced with the choice of continuing on the 45-mile route, or detouring to do the extra challenges of the 56-miler. To stay on the shorter option, cross Empire Grade, descend (and climb a little) for 2.7 miles on Ice Cream Grade to Pine Flat Road, and turn right.

To add the extra miles, turn left on Empire Grade for 3.5 miles, then right on Smith Grade for the five-mile descent to Bonny Doon Road. Turn

119

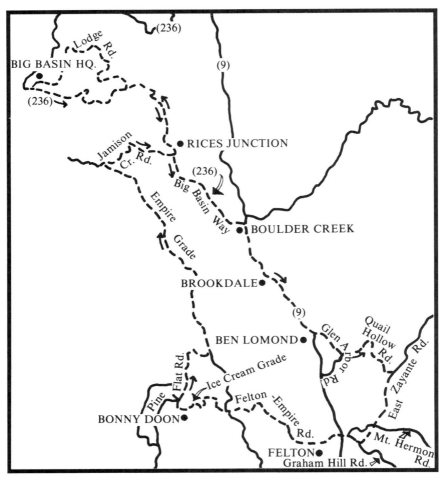

right on Bonny Doon and continue on Pine Flat at Ice Cream Grade, where you'll be back on the regular route.

You'll quickly discover that Pine Flat Road really isn't, but it's a mostly gradual climb for two miles back to Empire Grade. Turn left on Empire and enjoy the mostly rolling terrain — lots of easy-going climbs interspersed with dips — for the next six miles to Jamison Creek Road.

You may want to stop at the top of Jamison Creek Road for a snack or lunch. While you're at it, put on a windbreaker and prepare yourself mentally for the next three miles. Jamison Creek has a reputation as one of the most "interesting" descents in the Santa Cruz Mountains. According to Grant Peterson in *Roads to Ride South,* "No road this steep is great fun to descend, because you find yourself more concerned about controlling your speed and making the turns than you are with the joys of fast, effortless riding." Me, I've been known to stop as many as three times to cool my rims and catch my breath!

You'll get about a mile of easier going at the bottom of Jamison Creek before the road ends at Highway 236. Turn left for what now will seem like a trivial climb back toward Big Basin. In a little over three miles, look for the turn onto Lodge Road on your right. From here on in, just relax and enjoy the easy climbing, truly effortless downhills and beautiful scenery.

The first mile or so is an easy up, with only the lumpy patchwork pavement to distract you. After you cross the park boundary at the top, you'll have about another mile of downhill on the same patchwork. Finally, you'll roll onto better surface for the last three miles, passing through redwoods, madrones and oaks and rounding blind turns marked with "Sound Horn" signs. I agree with Grant when he says, "This is the type of road that you'll wish would go on for miles and miles."

Before you reach the end, you'll pass Sempervirens Falls on the left. It can be easy to miss through the dense forest, so keep an eye out for the fenced walkway down to the bottom. To get the full effect of the ribbon-like falls and the deep pool it fills, leave your bike at the sign and walk the few yards down. It's worth the stop!

Finally, about half a mile farther, you'll end up at Highway 236 again, across from Blooms (no relation) Creek Campground. Unless you want to turn around and do Lodge Road again, turn right and ride the mile and a half back to Big Basin Park Headquarters. You've met the Big Basin Mini-Challenge, Revised!

ROUTE SLIP

From Big Basin State Park Headquarters

TURN	ON	FOR
East	Highway 236	8.0
Right	Highway 9	3.75
Left	Glen Arbor Road	1.0
Left	Quail Hollow Road	4.75
Right	East Zayante Road	2.0
Right	Graham Hill Road	0.5
	Food and water in Felton	
Continue	Felton-Empire Road	3.75

Short Option:

	Cross Empire Grade to	
Continue	Ice Cream Grade	2.7
Right	Pine Flat Road	2.0

Long Option:

Left	Empire Grade	3.5
Right	Smith Grade	5.0
Right	Bonny Doon Road	3.3
Continue	Pine Flat Road	2.0
	At Ice Cream Grade	

Both:

Left	Empire Grade	6.0
Right	Jamison Creek Road	3.0
	Caution! Steep descent!	
Left	Highway 236	3.2
Right	Lodge Road	5.0
Right	Highway 236	1.5
	To Park Headquarters	

A Ride on the Wilder Ranch Side
May 1991

Mountain biking and beautiful scenery go together like pedals and toe clips. So it's sometimes hard to come up with impressive enough adjectives for a ride that features sights more spectacular than your run-of-the-mill, gee-whiz canyon vista. This is one of those rides.

This mountain biking paradise is just a mile or so north of Santa Cruz on Highway 1, at the relatively new Wilder Ranch State Park. A State Historical Park and cultural preserve, the old ranch is a "living history" museum. But for mountain bikers (and hikers and equestrians, we hasten to add) the park is a lot more.

Riding out from the ranch house area, you can pedal up steep dirt trails, follow single-track through redwoods, and come out in full sight of the Pacific Ocean, complete with seal rocks, kelp beds and crashing surf.

Of course, an incursion of coastal fog can cancel all this hyperbole. On the other hand, if the fog is thin enough to allow a modicum of visibility, it can turn the day into an even more aesthetic experience. High winds can keep the fog at bay all day, but they can also make some of the riding an extra-strenuous challenge.

Those driving to the park should be warned that State Parks charge a whopping $6.00 per car as of 1991 to park on their hallowed asphalt. If you're unwilling to pay that much, you can park on Highway 1 and ride into the park or simply ride your bike the mile and a half or so north from Santa Cruz.

The ranger at the entry station will be glad to give you a copy of a trail map, but don't rely on it to get you around. The map you see here is based on one drawn up for a combined horse/bike/hike event held in June 1990, and although it's much better, you'll probably still get lost. No sweat! Although the trails can cover great distances, you can be virtually certain that uphill is away from the highway, and downhill will eventually get you back to the ranch.

The easiest way to get to a trail is through the historical preserve. Keep going past the ranch house, the car barn and the picnic area on the trail that ducks through a short tunnel. On the other side of Highway 1, you'll see a big horse corral on your right.

Here you can bear right around the corral and continue up along the property line for Gray Whale Ranch. It's basically an out-and-back, which

you'll discover once you've circled around the high meadows a few times. On the way back down, you'll find plenty of single-track challenge on the double-track jeep trail. Don't let that magnificent ocean view distract you too much; pick your track carefully!

If you skip the out-and-back, make the hairpin left turn at the corral and climb to the Overlook, another great vista opportunity. From there you continue up

Super ocean views await you on Old Cove Landing Trail.

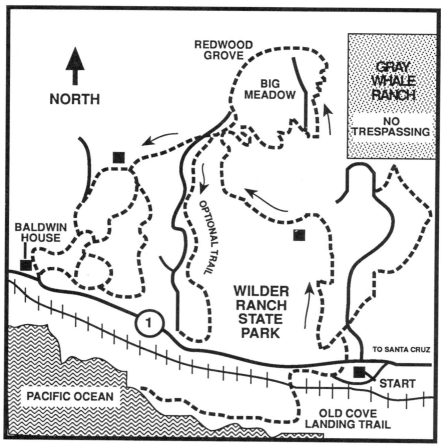

(and I do mean up!) to the Big Meadow junction. Here's where it's easiest to get lost by picking up the wrong trail. All that crisscrossing of road and trail looks nothing like any map available. Just realize that if you take the middle trail down to the equestrian staging area, it's STEEP, boggy, and sometimes totally absent. And the only way out is via Highway 1 or back up that mess.

The Big Meadow Loop gives you a chance to explore redwood forest on single track. You'll lose sight of the ocean for a while, but when you pop back out of the loop, there it is again, big as life! This is a good place to just pull up and find a comfy spot on a rock or patch of grass for a snack and some photo opportunities. (Did you remember to bring your binoculars?)

You can now head back downhill and enjoy one or more of the various loops between the equestrian trail and Baldwin House, an undeveloped old ranch site at the northern edge of the State Park property. If you intend to return to the ranch area via Baldwin House and Highway 1, you'll have a locked chain link gate to negotiate. Otherwise, you can just head back up and/or around to the Overlook, and then down to the tunnel.

Wilder Ranch is horse country. So remember to mind your best Ps and Qs out there. We've met up with cowboys from Gray Whale Ranch looking for strays, and with members of the Park's volunteer horse patrol.

Regardless of whether or not you seek higher ground, be sure to check out the Cultural Preserve, where you can take a guided or self-walking tour to learn more about the original Wilder Ranch. A working ranch and dairy from Spanish land grant days to the 1970s, it was home to four generations of Wilders for nearly a century. Now docents in period costumes share old-time activities with visitors. When we visited in June 1991, they greeted us with, "We'll be making old-fashioned lemonade and churning butter later. Come back after your ride!"

A fine way to finish off a Wilder Ranch ride is on two-mile Old Cove Landing Nature Trail, which runs along the ocean between the fields of brussels sprouts and the sea cliffs. Look for snowy plovers, cormorants, pelicans, harbor seals, and sea otters dining on shellfish in the kelp beds. You'll also discover a splendid fern grotto you can explore if the tide's well out (but leave your bike on the cliff!), and an impressive natural bridge.

Pick up a Cove Landing trail guide at the kiosk next to the restrooms on the far side of the parking lot, and follow the trail signs beyond. You'll descend to and cross the railroad tracks before beginning the nature trail section. Then the going is flat and fairly obvious until you get to the end, just beyond the grotto and natural bridge overlook. To return, reverse your direction and ride back along the water.

Now for some of that lemonade!

ROUTE SLIP

From Wilder Ranch parking lot

TURN	ON
Left	Paved path to ranch
Left	Ranch house driveway
	Continue through barnyard past picnic tables
Left	Into tunnel
	Crosses under Highway 1
Straight	Past Cowboy House
	Horse corral on right
Left	First trail junction
	Sharp hairpin, uphill
Straight	Wilder Overlook
	Stop and enjoy the view!

Bear right	Big Meadow junction
Right	Onto single track
Bear right	Toward Baldwin House
	Stop and enjoy the view!
or	
Bear Left	To loop back to Big Meadow

Return either via Overlook or down to Equestrian Staging Area.

Tour de Santa Cruz
October 1984

This ride originally appeared as "UC Santa Cruz: City on a Hill" in a column entitled "Academic Delights, Rides around the University."

College campuses offer cycle tourists some special joys of riding. Unique architecture, magnificent views and great people-watching beckon. Getting frustrated about learning your way around a new campus? Jump on your bike and take a ride. You'll quickly discover easier routes off the beaten (motorist) path.

This 40-mile + ride offers a full "tour de Santa Cruz" as well as a campus excursion. There's one major climb, up into the redwoods above Soquel, and another, slightly gentler one on the UC Santa Cruz campus. Built around the "cluster college" concept (as is England's Oxford University), UCSC resembles a community of several neighborhoods, thus the nickname "City on a Hill."

Starting from Cabrillo College's parking lot on the south side of Soquel Drive in Aptos, ride south on Cabrillo College Drive. At Park Avenue, turn left and cross under the freeway toward Capitola. Make a right on Kennedy Drive and continue on Monterey Avenue, following it as it turns left to descend to the beach and downtown Capitola. Turn right on busy Capitola Avenue, then bear left on Stockton and cross the bridge over Soquel Creek.

Here you have two climbs in front of you. Take the one on the right, Wharf Road, and enjoy the view of Loma Prieta to the east as you crank up past the Shadowbrook Restaurant. Follow Wharf around to the right and ride down into Soquel, turning right again at Robertson Road.

At the bottom, turn left on Porter Street and cross Soquel Drive at the light. Now you're on Old Soquel-San Jose Road and beginning your climb to the redwoods. In about four miles you'll arrive at Casalegno's store. There's more climbing ahead, so you may want to stop for a drink or snack.

Turn left on Laurel Glen Road and enjoy the relatively easy climb for about three more miles. Once it becomes Mountain View Road, the climbing gets tougher until you top out at the end of Rodeo Gulch Road.

Then you'll drop quickly to Branciforte Drive for the long downhill into Santa Cruz.

The road continues as Market Street, from which you'll turn right on Water Street. Cross the San Lorenzo River and continue on Mission Street past the downtown area and Pacific Garden Mall (both barely reviving from the 1989 quake). Just after crossing Highway 1, make a sharp right on Highland Avenue, then a left on High Street for the gentle climb to the UCSC campus.

Turn right at the Main Gate at the top of Bay Street and ride up until you see the signs for the campus bike path. Turn left onto the path and climb to the top of the hill. At the steepest point, the uphill side of the path veers off to the right, allowing the downhillers to maintain speed, while you get to ease up a bit.

The bike path will deliver you to the road accessing University House and the School of Performing Arts. Turn left, and at the intersection turn left again on Heller Drive to descend toward the Married Student Housing complex and the marvelous view of Monterey Bay. At the West Gate, turn left on Empire Grade.

Now it's on to Natural Bridges State Beach by the most direct route, down Western Drive. The descent is steep and was once in bad repair, but now it's well paved for smooth going all the way. Cross Highway 1 (it's not a freeway here) and turn right on Mission, then left on Natural Bridges Drive. A left on Delaware and right on Swanton will bring you to the entrance of the park.

Natural Bridges once boasted at least two of those marvelous phenomena, but they were destroyed in the heavy storms of the early 1980s. The beach is still a nice one, though, with plenty of picnic tables on the cliffs above, not to mention the most practical of bike tour stops, restrooms.

Another feature of the park is the eucalyptus grove that annually attracts swarms of Monarch butterflies who spend the winter soaking up the California sun on the trees' aromatic bark.

Leaving Natural Bridges, ride straight onto West Cliff Drive. You'll have a choice of a bike path or the road, but keep in mind that both can offer heavy traffic, either from cars or from rollerbladers, skateboarders and baby strollers. You'll soon pass the Mark Abbott Memorial Lighthouse and Steamer Lane, one of California's most exciting surfing spots.

At Pacific Street, turn right, then make a right onto Front Street. Another right puts you on Laurel Street Extension, which crosses the river to San Lorenzo Boulevard. Continue on East Cliff Drive and cross the next bridge to Murray, which becomes Eaton. You can circle the Yacht Harbor by turning right on Lake Avenue. Then turn left on East Cliff again, being very careful in the heavy traffic at the harbor parking lot entrance.

Follow East Cliff when it makes a sharp right at the Cheese Factory for

a beautiful ride along the Monterey Bay shoreline. At the end of East Cliff, jog left on 41st Avenue, then right onto Opal Cliff Drive. Turn right on Portola Road and you'll find yourself at the top of the hill you turned away from when you climbed out of Capitola. The view from here is worth a stop.

At the bottom, turn right on the Esplanade. Stop at Polar Bear Ice Cream on the corner if you're in the mood for a treat. Try the Bear Paw ice cream sandwich (ask for a Turkey Paw if you like coffee ice cream!). Then continue on Esplanade and turn left on Monterey. It's a climb, and traffic is heavy on weekends.

Cross the railroad tracks at the top and turn right on Park Avenue to pass above New Brighton State Beach. Continue on Park across the Highway 1 freeway and turn right on Cabrillo College Drive to return to your start.

ROUTE SLIP

From Cabrillo College Parking Lot, Cabrillo College Drive and Soquel Drive in Aptos

TURN	ON	FOR
Left	Cabrillo College Drive	1.0
Left	Park Avenue	0.25
Right	Kennedy Drive	0.25
Continue	Monterey Avenue	0.6
Left	Monterey Avenue	0.25
Right	Capitola Avenue	0.1
Left	Stockton - over bridge	< 0.1

Bear right	Wharf Road	1.5
Right	Soquel Wharf Road at Robertson	0.2
Left	Porter Street	0.40
Continue	Old Soquel-San Jose Road	4.0
Left	Laurel Glen Road at Casalegno's	2.8
Continue	Mountain View Road	1.0
Left/Continue	Branciforte Drive	6.75
Continue	Market Street	1.0
Right	Water Street	0.75
Continue	Mission Street/Highway 1	0.1
Sharp right	Highland Avenue	0.2
Left	High Street	1.4
Right	Bay Street/UCSC Main Gate	± 0.3
Left	Bike Path	1.5
Left	At end	0.10
Left	Meyer Drive	0.2
Left	Heller Drive	0.75
Left	Empire Grade at West Gate	1.0
Right	Western Drive	1.6
Right	Mission Street (beyond Highway 1)	0.1
Left	Natural Bridges Drive	0.5
Left	Delaware Street	0.2
Right	Swanton	0.25
Right	Into Natural Bridges State Beach	
Reverse	Out of Natural Bridges State Beach	
Continue	West Cliff Drive or bike path	3.5
Right	Pacific Street	0.1
Right	Front Street	0.2
Right	Laurel Street over bridge	0.2
Right	San Lorenzo Boulevard	0.4
Continue	East Cliff Drive	0.5
Left	Murray (becomes Eaton)	0.7
Right	Lake Avenue around Yacht Harbor	0.5
Left	East Cliff Drive	0.8
Right	East Cliff Drive at Cheese Factory	2.25
Left	41st Avenue	< 0.1
Immed. Right	Opal Cliff Drive	0.8
Right	Portola Drive	0.5
Right	Esplanade	0.1
Left	Monterey	0.2
Right	Park Avenue	1.5
Right	Cabrillo College Drive	1.0
Right	Into parking lot	

Exploring Steinbeck Country
November 1984

Between Watsonville, where *The Red Pony* was born, and King City, just *East of Eden*, lies the rich, fertile Salinas Valley that John Steinbeck described so eloquently. Although high-tech companies have threatened to move to Salinas, there's still much of the early 20th Century evident in the Valley. Long, flat country roads offer easy riding, handsome Victorian architecture, and acres of farmland for relaxed cycle touring. Hill climbing enthusiasts can also find a few challenges — and downhill thrills — on the slopes of Mount Toro.

If you want to explore Steinbeck country, you can include both kinds of riding on an extended 65-mile tour. Or you can stick to the 50+ miles of flat, but be warned that you'll probably encounter stiff winds, even if there's no storm raging out beyond Monterey Bay.

A burro on Corral de Tierra Road finds an easy-reach "feed bag."

You may want to take a picnic lunch to eat at Mount Toro Regional Park. You can buy your supplies at the start of this ride, from the shops that surround the intersection of Main Street (Hwy. 68) and Blanco Road in Salinas.

The most significant person I want to thank for introducing me to Salinas Valley's charms is Tom Thompson. In a way, this ride is dedicated to his memory. Inspiration also came from the Monterey Loop Century, which included Corral de Tierra.

To reach the starting point drive south on U.S. 101 to Salinas and take the Highway 68/John Street exit toward Monterey. From Highway 1 on Monterey Peninsula, take Highway 68 to Salinas. Park at one of the shopping centers at the corner of Blanco Road, just north of the freeway part of Highway 68.

Once on your bike, ride west on West Blanco Road toward Fort Ord. Start early or you'll encounter the winds from the bay on the way out to Reservation Road. You'll pass farmland in all stages of the planting cycle, from fallow to harvest. Crop dusters may buzz you, a reminder that the farmhouses along the road are only artifacts of the Victorian era.

Just before Reservation Road, you'll leave the farmland and enter the outskirts of Fort Ord, climbing up toward the East Garrison boundary through terrain that looks like it belongs in the Mojave Desert. Turn left on Reservation, and you'll soon be descending again, with a sweeping view of the Valley, its green fields a sharp contrast to the arid desert you just left. Near Davis Road, "The Bluffs" on your right look like eroded desert monuments.

To visit Toro Regional Park, turn right on Highway 68. The freeway ends almost immediately, and bikes are allowed. The park is about half a mile from the intersection, and it offers picnic areas, restrooms and water. If you're not stopping or taking the hilly detour, continue across the freeway onto River Road.

Hilly Detour

On the other hand, if you're up for a climb on Mount Toro, keep going beyond the park for about four miles. If you look up to your left just before San Benancio Road, you'll see the road you'll eventually descend. Pass San Benancio and turn left onto Corral de Tierra Road.

In just over two miles you'll come to Four Corners, where Corral de Tierra makes a sharp left. Take it and begin the gradual, rolling climb through some of the Valley's most beautiful ranch land. You'll enjoy the shade of the trees, some forming "tunnels" over the road.

After about six miles of this gradual climb, turn left on San Benancio Road, where you really get to climb — for about 0.2 miles! The top is about as high as you can get on the mountain and stay on the road. Now you'll have over four miles of downhill back to Highway 68. Turn right on Highway 68 to return to the "flatlander" route on River Road.

Tailwind along the River

Riding the nine miles of easy, rolling terrain to the Chualar Bridge, you'll soon be racing along with the wind at your back, past well-kept

Arabians and quarter horses and lots more agriculture.

At the one-lane bridge marked Chualar River Road, turn left and cross over the Salinas River. The road turns left again, then right. In about two miles you'll cross over U.S. 101 to the village of Chualar. Food and drink have a distinctly south-of-the-border flavor here. Turn left on Grant, then right on Payson at the end of town.

Payson becomes Chualar Road for two miles to Old Stage Road. Turn left here and you'll find yourself headed into the wind again. In about four and a half miles Old Stage Road makes a sharp right turn at the junction with Alisal Road. Take the right and continue for another eight miles to Natividad. Here's where the abundance of the Valley really becomes apparent. Fields of cabbage, cauliflower, zucchini and more stretch out on either side of the road and continue right into town.

Make a left onto Old Natividad Road, then left again onto Natividad Road. In about four miles you'll encounter your first traffic light since you left town at the start of your ride. Continue to Laurel Drive and make another left turn. From here you'll have a clear view of Mount Toro at the opposite end of the Valley.

At the next light, turn right on Sanborn Road and cross through the main part of town. In about three miles Sanborn becomes East Blanco Road at Abbott Street. Continue along Blanco to Main Street, and the end of your Salinas Valley tour.

ROUTE SLIP

From Blanco Road and Main Street (Highway 68) in Salinas

TURN	ON	FOR
West	Blanco Road	7.5
Left	Reservation Road	13.0
	Becomes River Road at Highway 68	

Hilly Option:

Right	Highway 68	4.5
	Toro Regional Park in about 0.5 mi. - water, restrooms	
Left	Corral de Tierra Road	2.0
Left	Corral de Tierra Road	6.0
	At Four Corners	
Left	San Benancio Road	4.5
Right	Highway 68	4.0
Right	River Road	8.0

Both:

Left	Chualar River Road	2.0
Left	Grant	< 0.1

Right	Payson	2.0
	Becomes Chualar Road	
Left	Old Stage Road	4.5
Right	Old Stage Road at Alisal Road	8.0
Left	Old Natividad Road	0.1
Left	Natividad Road	5.4
Left	Laurel Drive	2.0
Right	Sanborn Road	3.0
Continue	East Blanco Road to Main Street	2.0

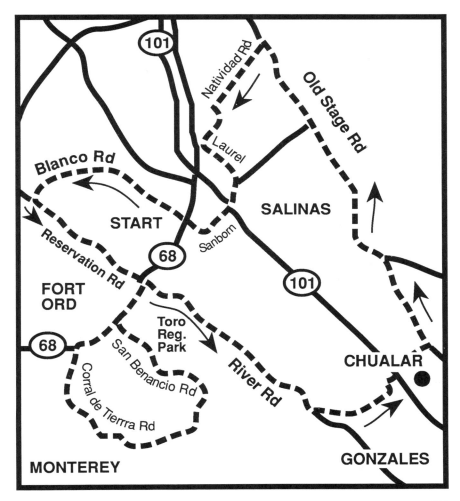

On the Mission Trail to San Juan Bautista

November 1989

Here's a ride that's somehow managed to escape the attention of all those "tours of the Bay Area" books on the shelf at your local bike shop. And that's a shame, because the roads between San Juan Bautista and Elkhorn Slough offer some history, some nature study, and, except for a narrow corridor along U.S. 101 and Highway 156, minimal traffic.

So the next sunny weekend when you realize you're tired of the same old routes and the same old sights, load your bikes on the car and head south on U.S. 101. Drive beyond Gilroy and take Highway 156 toward San Juan Bautista. Park anywhere on or off San Juan Canyon Road just south of town and take off from there. You'll be heading to Aromas and Prunedale, where you can find food and drink, but better fill your water bottles before you leave home.

The trick to this ride is to do it in the right direction, keeping the prevailing northwesterly winds behind you for as much of the 45-mile route as possible. That's one reason I altered the original route created by Walter and Liane McCabe for the Western Wheelers' Long Distance Training Group. (But, please, don't blame me if the winds turn on you in anticipation of changing weather!)

Start riding on Highway 156 and circle the town on Lucy Brown Road and San Justo Road to Anzar Road, which takes you under U.S. 101. Now you'll be climbing gradually for about four miles into the Aromas hills. On Carr Road, you'll suddenly plunge down about a mile of straight-as-an-arrow descent into Aromas. If it's Saturday and you're already hungry, the Ducky Deli on Blohm Avenue will probably be open.

Aromas is a little island of country culture surrounded by strawberry fields and pastureland. Last spring, on our training ride, the aroma of field-ripening strawberries lent credence to the community's name. Unfortunately, much of the farmland is giving way to development, so enjoy it while it lasts.

Aromas and San Juan Roads will take you out of Aromas toward Monterey Bay, then via Tarpey, San Miguel Canyon and Hall to Elkhorn Road. Riding south on Elkhorn, you'll be paralleling the estuary and salt marshes of Elkhorn Slough National Estuarine Sanctuary.

Once the mouth of the Salinas River (before man and nature both contrived to turn the river farther south), Elkhorn Slough mingles fresh and salt waters in a unique habitat for geoduck clams, leopard sharks, bat rays and more species of birds than possibly anywhere else on the California coast. You can make a stop at the Visitor Center here, but even if you don't, you'll probably be able to spot several different birds from the seat of your bike.

We'll come back to Elkhorn Road for another tour of the slough. For now, though, it's time to head for Prunedale and some lunch. Take Strawberry Road out to San Miguel Canyon and the busy shopping center just off U.S. 101. For the first time since leaving San Juan Bautista, you'll need to be concerned with traffic.

You can choose from a deli, a Mexican cantina and a supermarket here. If you'd rather buy (or carry from home) the makings of a picnic, head back up San Miguel Canyon to Echo Valley Road on your right. Turn left on Maher Road and climb up to Royal Oaks Park, which has all the picnic ground amenities you'll need.

After lunch, back on San Miguel Canyon at 101, reverse your direction to Castroville Boulevard. Look for Paradise Road on your right and take it to cut over to Elkhorn on Bay View and Walker Valley.

Turn right on Elkhorn and ride the length of the slough back north. Then cut over to San Miguel Canyon on Garin and Lewis, and proceed back to San Juan Road, where you can make the most of the tailwind chasing you back to Aromas! From here you'll be retracing your tracks to San Juan Bautista.

Once you reach town, turn left onto Second Street, right onto Franklin, and left onto Alameda and ride to Mission San Juan Bautista. Here's where your bike tour ends and your history tour begins. The old plaza surrounding the Mission is a State Historical Park featuring replicas of the original town hotel, jail and blacksmith shop. There's also an earthquake display, complete with seismograph, where you can stand over the San Andreas Fault line.

The Mission itself is the largest in California and has served as a movie set. Alfred Hitchcock fans may or may not recognize the set for the final scene from Vertigo (the missing element is a tower that was "pasted" onto the building via film editing and special effects).

There are still more attractions to tiny San Juan Bautista. You can satisfy any bikie appetite at the Mexican restaurants along Alameda and its side streets. Or sample some of the Portuguese specialities at the San Juan Bakery, which claims to be the oldest continuously operating establishment of its kind in California.

For hard-hitting riders who'd rather make a long, steep ascent to earn those extra calories, there's always the 2,969-foot climb to Fremont Peak. Just head south on San Juan Canyon Road and keep climbing for the next 11 miles! Your reward at the top will be a 360° view, and a fast plunge back to San Juan and dinner.

If you'd rather skip the tough climb, you can still drive up to the top of the peak at dusk for a free look through the open-to-the-public telescope. If it's especially clear, or if the coastal fog is blocking the nearby city lights, you might just get a peek from the peak at the rings of Saturn.

ROUTE SLIP

From San Juan Canyon Road and Highway 156 in San Juan Bautista

TURN	ON	FOR
Left	Highway 156	1.80
Left	Lucy Brown Road	1.0
Left	San Justo	1.0
Right	San Justo	1.0
Left	San Juan Highway	0 .1
	Immediate turn to cross U.S. 101	
Right	Anzar	3.0
Right	Anzar	1.0
	At Cole	
Left	Carr	1.0
	Great downhill into Aromas!	
Right	Carpenteria	2.5
	Ducky Deli on right on Blohm Avenue	
Left	Aromas Road	1.0
Left	San Juan Road	1.0
Right	Tarpey	1.0
Straight	San Miguel Canyon	0.3
Right	Hall	2.25
Left	Elkhorn	3.0
	Slough and salt marshes on right	
Left	Strawberry	2.5
Left	San Miguel Canyon	2.0
	Caution! Heavy traffic!	
	Food and services in Prunedale	
	Royal Oak Park on Maher	
Right	San Miguel Canyon	0.25

Reverse direction:

Left	Castroville Boulevard	1.0
Right	Paradise	0.5
Left	Bay View	0.15
Right	Walker Valley	0.25
Left	Elkhorn	3.5
	More slough watching opportunities	
Right	Garin	1.5
Right	Lewis	1.5
Left	San Miguel Canyon	2.0
Right	San Juan Road	2.0
Left	Aromas Road	1.0
Left	Carpenteria	0.25
Left	Carr	1.0

Right	Anzar	4.0
Right	San Juan Highway	2.0
Left	Second	0.1
Right	Franklin	0.1
Left	Alameda	0.1
	To Mission and State Historical Park	

Hard Hitters' Side Trip To Fremont Peak:

Left	San Juan Highway	2.0
Continue	San Juan Canyon Road	9.0
	2900-foot climb!	
Reverse	San Juan Canyon Road to return to Highway 156	

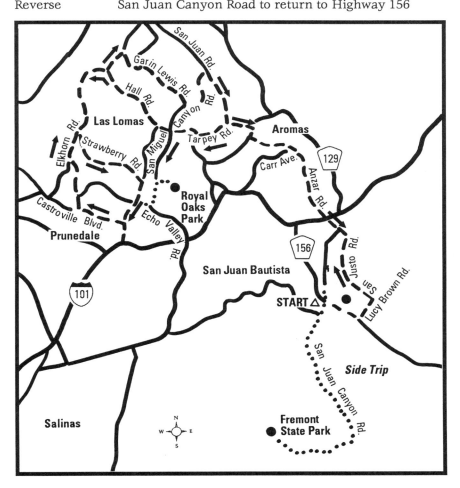

Salinas Valley's Perfect Country Road

March 1987

Sick of inhaling carbon monoxide fumes and bumping in and out of potholes? Weary of fighting heavy traffic just to get out to the country and ride a few miles? Frustrated when the traffic gets even worse once you do get out there?

Well, take heart. Spring is just about the best time of the year to load the bikes on the rack and take off for the real countryside. Somewhere out there wildflowers are blooming and the air is fresh and clean. Somewhere out there waits the perfect country road — smoothly paved, surrounded by open space, drenched in California sunshine, and completely devoid of motor traffic!

Yes, Virgil and Virginia, there is such a road. It winds for some 36 miles through the southern Salinas Valley, including a patch of Hunter Liggett Military Reservation and two tiny dots on the map known as Jolon and Lockwood. A side trip to Mission San Antonio adds a flat and interesting eleven miles to your ride.

I discovered the original loop on this tour some five years ago, when a friend and I set out to explore unknown territory south of King City. Although I've since been back in the area for a couple of century rides, I've never reridden this specific route.

A call to Sunstorm Cyclery down in Palo Robles assured me that there is still a country store in Lockwood. (I remember buying a full lunch there and eating it in an empty field around the corner.) But the shop owner was unable to confirm all my directions. So please forgive me if you find you should have made a right turn instead of a left somewhere on this ride. If you have a map, you can't get completely lost — there are only so many ways to cross U.S. 101 and the Salinas River!

Driving down, take U.S. 101 south to King City, exit at Jolon Road and continue south to San Lucas Road, the best place to start. We parked at a tavern about a mile beyond the intersection, but I have no idea if it's still there. So be sure to fill your water bottles before striking out in search of your best starting spot.

Once on your bikes, ride south on Jolon Road for about eleven miles. You'll have a short uphill climb, followed by a breezy downhill into Hunter Liggett. One of the first things you'll notice that's a bit different from the outside world is the kind of messages painted on the road. Instead of words like "Stop Ahead," you'll read: "Caution — Tank Crossing!"

You'll also notice the high quality of the pavement. Potholes, debris and uneven patch jobs are totally missing. Yet there's no real traffic to speak of. As long as there are no maneuvers under way, you can expect the ride to remain smooth and tranquil for the entire loop.

Mission San Antonio, 5.5 miles from Jolon Road in Hunter Liggett Military Reservation.
Photo courtesy of Mission San Antonio.

If you'd like to visit historic Mission San Antonio, turn right on Mission Road and ride 5.5 miles farther into the reservation. (I was amazed when I saw that 5.5 miles on the map. It's so flat and goes by so fast, I could have sworn it was only a couple of miles!) At the end of the road, you'll find a pleasant retreat surrounded by flower gardens, peace and quiet.

Reverse your direction and ride the same 5.5 miles back out to Jolon Road to pick up the loop again. You'll have six more miles to cover before reaching Lockwood, where you'll find the country store.

Once you turn left on Lockwood-San Lucas Road, the terrain will begin to change from ranches and grazing land to undeveloped range filled with native plants. You'll climb through San Lucas Canyon, and the higher you get, the more impressive the view, culminating with the Pinnacles to the northeast, across the Salinas River. Then you'll shoot down toward the river and cross U.S. 101 to Paris Valley Road.

Turn left onto Paris Valley Road, then left again onto Oasis Road for about three miles. Where Oasis turns right, back north toward King City, you bear left to pick up San Lucas Road for another three miles back to Jolon Road.

Should you want to make a full weekend out of your journey south, here's a second day's ride of about 50 rather hilly miles, a scenic loop once featured on the Twin Lakes Century out of Paso Robles:

Ride south 22 miles from Lockwood on Interlake Road (G14), all the way around San Antonio Reservoir, and within sight of Lake Nacimiento. To return, make a left on Nacimiento Lake Drive (G19), ride twelve miles toward U.S. 101, turn left once again onto Jolon Road (G18), and finish with about 15 miles back up to Lockwood. Be sure you have low gears and strong legs before starting out on this one!

Because the lakes are popular for all sorts of water recreation, you'll probably encounter quite a bit of traffic, including boat trailers. Be patient: you'll soon be back on the southern stretch of Jolon Road. And after five years of exploring the back roads of central and northern California, I still believe it's the perfect country road!

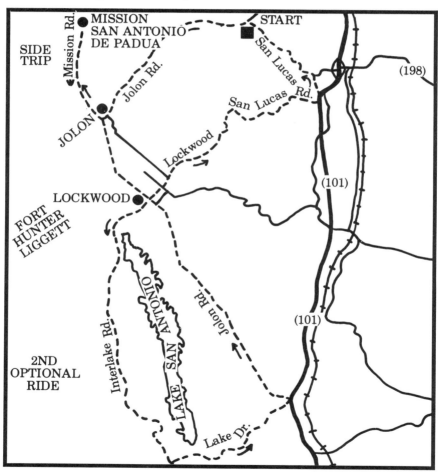

ROUTE SLIP

From Jolon Road and San Lucas Road, off U.S. 101 south of King City

TURN	ON	FOR
South	Jolon Road	11.2

Optional Side Trip to Mission San Antonio:

Right	Mission Road	5.5
Reverse	Mission Road	5.5
Right	Jolon Road	

All:

Left	Lockwood-San Lucas Road	14.0
	Country store	
Left	Paris Valley Road	1.3
Left	Oasis Road	3.0
Bear Left	San Lucas Road	3.0
	To Jolon Road	

6. SIERRA NEVADA
Tahoe to Yosemite

Welcome to the rewards of high-altitude cycling: the scenic environments of Lake Tahoe and Yosemite, the challenge of high mountain passes, and the ensuing high-speed descents. Best of all, they're accompanied by fresh air and cool temperatures that add to the pleasure of every ride, whether you're on your way to witness a legendary race or the granite record of high Sierra glaciation. Enjoy!

Tahoe's Most Spectacular Downhill: The Brockway Summit Loop
September 1986

September is a magic month in the Lake Tahoe basin. Summer is at its peak, with bright, warm, sunny days strung out one right after another. The kids have all gone back to school, and the "summer folk" have fled back to the city. The mobs of skiers that follow the snow won't be around for at least two more months, and traffic is at an all-time low. It's the perfect time for pedal touring.

This 40-mile loop connecting Lake Tahoe with Truckee adds another bit of magic to the September formula: one of the most spectacular downhill rides I've found anywhere — four miles straight as an arrow from Brockway Summit through Martis Valley into Truckee!

When I was a kid, I always saved the best part of any treat for last. Nowadays, I tend to do the same for a ride like this. I start from Truckee and ride up the river canyon to Tahoe City, around the lake to King's Beach and up to the summit. Then I get to do that wonderful downhill at the end. Starting from any other location along the way, however, won't spoil your fun a bit.

A good place to start is Donner Memorial State Park, just off Highway 80, one exit west of Truckee. There's plenty of parking, water and bathrooms, plus some interesting historical exhibits. From the park, turn right on Donner Pass Road and cross the freeway to ride east into Truckee. In town, make a right onto Lake Tahoe Boulevard, which becomes State Highway 89 in about a quarter of a mile.

Continue south on 89 up the Truckee River canyon. The road climbs gently along the river through the Tahoe National Forest. If you start early in the morning, be prepared for this part of the ride to be downright cold. The sun will not rise above the hills east of the river until almost midmorning, so take along a warm jacket or windbreaker, cap and full gloves.

In about eight miles, you'll come to the Squaw Valley turn-off on the right. You'll find a 7-11 and a cafe here at the intersection. A highly recommended deli and the Granite Chief Bike Shop are about two miles further up the Squaw Valley Road.

It's another mile and a half to the Alpine Meadows turn-off, and the River Ranch Inn. This is the "put out" place for rafters floating down the Truckee River. The hamburgers here are fairly tasty, and if you stop to eat, you can watch the action from the patio while dining *al fresco.*

This is also where the two-way Tahoe City bike path begins. You'll find it to the right of the highway, paralleling both the road and the river on a contour line between the two. It's well graded and maintained from here to town and offers a closer view of the river. In early spring and late fall, watch out for slippery ice patches; if there are a lot of them, you might be better off sticking to the road.

Both road and bike path will bring you into Tahoe City at the junction of Highway 89, which turns right over the river toward South Lake Tahoe, and Highway 28, which proceeds north along the lake. You might want to check out the action on "Fanny Bridge" (observe the folks leaning out over the water and you'll see where the name comes from). Occasionally you can see fish leaping up the special ladder on the dam at the lake's outlet to the river, just beyond the bridge.

Go straight at the traffic light onto Highway 28, North Lake Boulevard, and ride through town. If you haven't eaten yet, you'll find a plethora of restaurants. There are also two excellent bike shops right on North Lake Boulevard—one at the back of Basecamp on the inland side, and Olympic Bike Shop on the lake side.

You can pick up the bike path again, on the right, just outside of town. But if you're like me, you'll choose the road rather than the bumpy terrain and frequent interruptions on the path, which I've enjoyed only on my mountain bike. You'll begin climbing just before Lake Forest, and the going gets steeper as you advance. In two miles and 250 feet of elevation gain, you'll be atop Dollar Hill, with a sweeping vista of the north end of the lake before you: Carnelian Bay, Agate Bay and Crystal Bay dropping into your line of sight and sparkling in the sunlight. You can keep them in sight almost all the way down the other side into Cedar Flat.

From the top of Dollar Hill to Kings Beach is just over six miles, most of it downhill or flat. There's more food in Kings Beach, including a great little bakery just beyond the Highway 267 turn-off. At the traffic light, turn left (north) onto 267, Northshore Boulevard, and gear down for the ascent to Brockway Summit.

The going gets pretty tough for about three miles, as you climb some 1300 feet up to 7179 feet at the top. Take a well-deserved breather here and

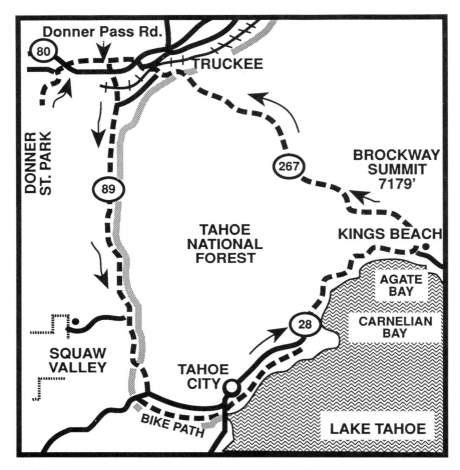

look back where you came from for another matchless view of Lake Tahoe.

The descent begins with a couple of short switchbacks. Then suddenly you're looking down a straight ribbon of highway, plunging four miles down to a flat plain that was once a lake but now supports the Northstar-at-Tahoe golf course and the Truckee-Tahoe Airport. Back off the brakes and let 'er rip!

(Friends of mine once equipped their tandem with a faring for this ride. When they reached the flat part of the road opposite the Truckee Airport, their speedometer read 57 miles per hour!)

You'll have another 4.7 miles of rolling terrain to use up the momentum you gathered on the downhill before you reach the last descent into Truckee. Now's the time to stop for a drink at the Bar of America (yes, the building was once a bank), or visit the bike shop behind the Alpenglow mountaineering store.

To return to Donner State Park, turn left (west) on Donner Pass Road and ride through town, cross Interstate 80, and turn left at the park entrance. A ride to the other end of Donner Lake and back could be a pleasant way to cool down after experiencing one of the greatest downhills in the High Sierra.

ROUTE SLIP

From Donner Memorial State Park

TURN	ON	FOR
Right	Donner Pass Road	1.0
	Cross Highway 80 into Truckee	
Right	Lake Tahoe Boulevard	14.0
	Becomes Highway 89	
	Squaw Valley on right in 8 miles	
	River Ranch on right in 9.5 miles; bike path begins	
Continue	North Lake Boulevard/Highway 28	10.0
	At Tahoe City Y	
	Check out the view from the top of Dollar Hill!	
Left	Northshore Boulevard/Highway 267	13.0
	Gear down!	
	Brockway Summit 3.0 miles	
Left	Donner Pass Road	2.5
Left	Donner State Park	

Tahoe to Nevada City
June 1989

I'll never forget my first bicycle race. The year was 1981, the day was a blazing hot Father's Day, and the race was the Nevada City Classic. The course twisted and turned up and down the steep streets of downtown Nevada City, some 33 times around a one-mile loop.

I immediately got caught up in the excitement as one kid, just barely old enough to race as a senior, lapped the entire field not once, but three times! That kid was Greg Lemond, and it was the last year he raced in Nevada City.

Today the 29-year-old Tour of Nevada City criterium is a National Prestige Classic that attracts some of the hottest teams and individual racers in the country. So even though you probably won't get to see Lemond wrap circles around the pack, it's still just about Northern California's most exciting race.

If you play your cards right, you can have your cake and eat it too on Father's Day weekend by combining a trip to Lake Tahoe with a day at the races. It does take a little advance planning, along with some basic bikie stamina (the kind that gets you up early in the morning to ride a century).

Make the trip to Tahoe Friday night, and go for a ride or a hike or just laze in the sun on Saturday. You can camp, but for comfort and convenience, I recommend renting a cabin on the North Shore, not too far from Tahoe City. Saturday night you can carboload on pasta at Lanza's in Carnelian Bay or at Josephine's in Truckee.

Get to bed early, though, because on Sunday morning, you'll have to rise and shine at oh-dark-thirty for the 63-mile ride to Nevada City. If you leave early enough, you should get there in time to witness all the drama of both the women's and the men's races.

Keep in mind that all cars driven up to the lake Friday night must get to Nevada City by the end of the day Sunday in order to ferry all the cyclists home after the races. It's a good idea to arrange for at least one car to serve as a sag wagon, especially between Interstate 80 and Highway 49, where water is hard to come by.

Before you leave Tahoe, eat a hot breakfast and don plenty of warm clothes in layers. Nothin's colder than riding down the Truckee Canyon before 8:00 a.m. But take cool clothing along. Nothin's hotter than pedaling over Washington Ridge on Highway 20 after 10:00 a.m. Oh yeah, better bring your granny along to bail you out on the long, steep climb over Donner Summit.

These directions start from the Y intersection of Highway 28 and Highway 89 in Tahoe City. It's a pretty straightforward exercise in navigation to get yourself there from wherever you're staying (all through-roads on the North Shore seem to lead to Tahoe City).

As you ride north through the canyon, keep reminding yourself that you'll warm up when you get to Donner Pass Road. It's a steep, switchbacky, three-mile climb to the summit. You'll thank old granny before you're through. Just gear all the way down to your triple and you'll simply spin up the hill. Look up as often as you can; the views of the surrounding peaks and Donner Lake below are spectacular. And you'll appreciate how the bridge at the summit keeps getting larger as you get closer to it.

Once you top out at Sugar Bowl Ski Area, you'll enjoy a fast ride down Old Highway 40 through Norden and Soda Springs. Almost anywhere along this four-mile stretch is a good place to meet up with riding companions who'd rather skip the hill, thanks. It's all downhill from here (except for the uphills, of course!). By the way, Soda Springs is your last opportunity to buy on-the-bike food before plunging down the mountain.

Pick up Old Donner Pass Road (still often called Old Highway 40) on the north side of Interstate 80. Paralleling the Emigrant Trail on your way

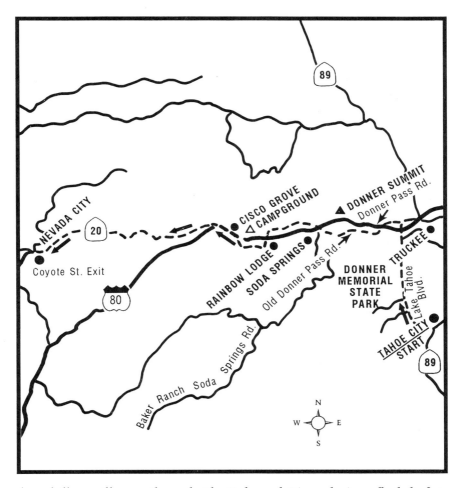

downhill, you'll pass through Pla Vada and Kingvale in a flash before crossing under the freeway onto Hampshire Rocks Road. Rainbow Lodge on your left and the Forest Service campground at Big Bend on your right are your last pit stop opportunities.

You'll cross back under the freeway onto Old Donner Pass Road, then zip through Cisco Grove. It's easy to miss the left turn onto the overpass here. So if you find yourself on the private road into the Thousand Trails Campground, turn around and turn right. The overpass will dump you onto Interstate 80 for about two miles of freeway ramps and shoulder.

Take the next exit onto Highway 20 to Nevada City for 27 more miles and the trip over Washington Ridge. There's no water along here, unless you detour to some of the Forest Service campgrounds. By now the temperature should be climbing steadily. You'll be glad to shed your warm gear and dive into the water coolers on your sag. Once everyone sheds and refills water bottles, send the sag ahead to grab a parking space in town before they're all gone.

You'll know you've reached Nevada City when Highway 20 becomes Highway 49. The first exit, Coyote Street, comes up instantly. Take it and look for your sag so you can lock up or stash your bikes, change your shoes and spend the rest of the day on foot.

You can walk the entire mile-long course — up and down the narrow, hilly streets of the main part of town — in just a few minutes. But you'll want to make plenty of stops to watch the racers struggle up the steep climbs, dash down the descents, and haul themselves around the sharp corners. Just don't stand too close to the hay bales on the side; they're there for a reason! There are often spectacular crashes.

You'll find plenty of *al fresco* restaurants along the course where you can grab lunch and still keep an eye on the action. And between passes of the pack, you'll find yourself talking to other folks gathered along the sidelines. You'll probably recognize quite a few of them, in fact. Nevada City on Father's Day is the place to run into those long-lost riding companions you haven't seen in years.

When the day ends, you'll be sunburned and weary, but completely recovered from your own ride. And who knows, you just may have been lucky enough to witness the challenge of some "unknown" kid as he or she charged out in front and held the lead by doubling laps on the pack. And wouldn't that be something to reminisce about when she (or he) becomes a world champion?

ROUTE SLIP

From the Y at the intersection of Highways 28 and 89 in Tahoe City

TURN	ON	FOR
North	Highway 89	14.0
Left	Over Interstate 80	1.0
Right	Donner Pass Road	3.5
Straight	Donner Pass Road	3.0
	At South Shore Drive	
Straight	Old Donner Pass Road	4.0
	At Sugar Bowl	
Left	Old Donner Pass Road	8.0
	Across Interstate 80	
	Cross Interstate 80 to Hampshire Rocks Road,	
	then again to Old Donner Pass Road	

Left	Onto bridge over Interstate 80	0.5
	At Cisco Grove	
	Do not enter Thousand Trails Camp!	
Right	Interstate 80	2.0
Right	Nevada City/Highway 20 Exit	27.0
Right	Coyote Street Exit	
	Enjoy the races!	

Fall in Yosemite
October 1989

Autumn, and the riding in Yosemite National Park is easy. Or at least it's a lot easier than it was a month or so ago. The mercury's already descending to more reasonable levels. The kids have all gone back to school, and the yuppies back to work. Even most of the Winnebago crowd have retired to winter resting places. Now's the time to head for the hills, after the rush, but before the rains and snows begin in earnest.

You can camp or lodge in Yosemite Valley if you like, but I prefer the down-home peace and quiet of Wawona, just five miles inside the park from the southern entrance. Staying here you can sleep late and simply spin up the five miles and 1,000 feet back to the Entrance Station and beyond to hike the Sequoia-lined trails of the Mariposa Grove. Or rise early and head out on this 56-mile round trip to Glacier Point and back.

To reach Wawona, take State Highway 99 south to Madera, where you pick up Highway 145 East. At Highway 41, turn left and drive into the foothills, through Oakhurst and Fish Camp to the park entrance. Turn left and descend to Wawona.

If you want to stay inside the park, you have three equally attractive options: camping, hotel or guest cottages. The camping is at Wawona Campground, right on Wawona Road (Highway 41), on the banks of the South Fork of the Merced River. Be sure to reserve in advance; even in autumn it fills up quickly. Same for the historic Wawona Hotel, which generally remains open through October. Call 209-252-4848 for reservations.

Two establishments rent cottages about a mile and a quarter down North Wawona Road. Contact The Redwoods at P.O. Box 2085, Wawona Station, Yosemite National Park, CA 95389, 209-375-6666 or Camp Chilnualna, Box 2095, Wawona, CA 95389, 209-375-6295. Otherwise, you'll find motels and lodges in both Fish Camp (2.5 miles from the Park Entrance) and Oakhurst (about 14 miles south of Fish Camp).

The ride to Glacier Point is one of my favorites. It's long enough to warrant a big meal at ride's end, but the roads are graded well enough to

149

ward off serious high-altitude anaerobic episodes. Not to mention that the turnaround is at perhaps the most spectacular overview of Yosemite Valley, and the return is capped by one heck of a terrific downhill!

Be sure to add some layers of clothing to your panniers for the higher altitudes you'll be attaining. If the weather shuts down, it could actually snow above Chinquapin junction. And take along plenty of water; although you'll be handy to the ranger station at Badger Pass and to Bridal Veil Campground just off Glacier Point Road, there's no guarantee that either will be open at this time of year.

The ride begins at Wawona Ranger Station, near the junction of Wawona Road (Highway 41) and Chilnualna Falls Road. You'll start climbing right away, and continue to do so for about seven miles. According to Randall Braun in his *Cyclists' Route Atlas: A Guide to the Gold Country & High Sierra/ South,* the grade never exceeds 5.8%, although it may feel like more as you gain altitude. The next two miles will be mostly rolling to flat, but after the nine-mile mark, you'll be climbing steadily again to the 6100-foot level, hard by the entrance to the Yosemite West condominiums. The last mile to Chinquapin, however, is all downhill!

At Chinquapin, turn right onto Glacier Point Road and climb the five miles to Badger Pass at 7300 feet. The first three miles or so are pretty steady slogging, but things ease up as you approach the turnoff to the

View of Half Dome from Glacier Point above Yosemite Valley.

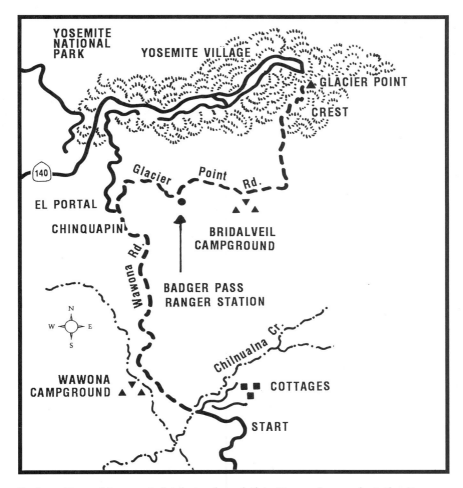

Badger Pass ski area (which is closed this time of year, but the Ranger Station will most likely be staffed).

Glacier Point is now a mere 11 miles away. The first mile or so will take you to the crest of the ridge between Badger and Summit Meadow. At the bottom of the descent, at the foot of the meadow, you'll find two (possibly welcome) pit toilets. It's another eight miles of mostly climbing to Bridal Veil Campground, where both toilets and water are available if the campground's open. The climb ends at the Sentinel Dome/Taft Point trailhead, which is on your left.

Now it's about a mile of downhill switchbacks to the first overlook above Glacier Point. Here you'll find excellent views of Vernal Falls, Half Dome, and Little Yosemite Valley. If you continue down the winding switchbacks to the concession stands, you'll be treated to even more spectacular views, plus a geology exhibit, snack bar and gift shop. You'll be tempted to stay for hours just enjoying the sights.

But keep in mind that the days are short in October, and you'll want to be back in Wawona before dark. So refill your water bottles, gear all the way down and tackle those switchbacks. (Last year, as we prepared to do just that, a woman with a deep Southern drawl asked us, "Are y'all really going to climb back out of here?")

It's not all that bad, really. Braun claims the two-mile ascent averages only 6%. But there are a couple of steep pitches to look out for! Once you reach the Sentinel/Taft trailhead, you'll have a long, pleasant descent that ends at Bridal Veil Creek. The rest of the ride to Badger is short rollers, culminating with the long downhill to Chinquapin. Then it's back up for a mile, and down all the way (yahoo!) to Wawona!

If you'd like to explore more Yosemite-area roads, Braun recommends the ride from Big Oak Flat to Hetch Hetchy. The climbs and descents are similar to those on the way to Glacier Point, but the altitude stays comfortably under 5000 feet.

ROUTE SLIP

From Wawona Ranger Station, Highway 41 and Chilnualna Falls Road in Wawona

TURN	ON	FOR
Right	Wawona Road/Highway 41	12.0
Right	Glacier Point Road	5.0
	At Chinquapin Junction	
Continue	Glacier Point Road	11.0
	At Badger Pass Turnoff	
	For Ranger Station, turn right	
Right	Upper Glacier Point Parking Lot	
	Check out the views!	
Continue	To Lower Parking Lot	
	More, better views!	
Reverse	Glacier Point Road	16.0
	Reverse trip to Chinquapin	
Left	Wawona Road/Highway 41	12.0

APPENDIX

Tools to Carry with You

As Angel Rodriguez tells the story . . .

One day I went down and got an ice cream cone (pecan-praline), and as I walked past the bus stop towards my bike, my friend Amy got off the bus. If you knew Amy you would have to stop and talk, especially if you saw her get off a bus. Amy rides her bike everywhere. I asked her what she was doing on the bus, and she proceeded to tell me about her theory of bike repair. It's a very simple theory: carry bus money and a bike lock. When your bike breaks down, lock it to something sturdy, take the bus home, get your car, go back to pick up the bike, and drop it off at your favorite bike shop. I was impressed. Not a spot of grease on her. Then I told her about my friend Herman.

When I first started cycling, Herman took us out on rides. Herman must have been forty or fifty at the time; hard for me to tell 'cause he still looks the same 14 years later. One day we were out riding, and my rear derailleur wasn't quite adjusted. And as it must always happen, I shifted into the spokes, tearing up my derailleur and breaking a few spokes – on the freewheel side, of course. I was ready to call Mom to come get me when Herman rolled up; he always seemed to be there when you needed him. He looked at the bike, said no problem, and unrolled his tool kit. Lo and behold, he had an extra rear derailleur, a few spokes of various lengths, a freewheel tool for every bike you could think of, plus a five-pound wrench to use on the freewheel tools. What a guy!

My conversation with Amy made me think about tool kits. Cyclists want to know, "What tools should I buy and when should I carry them?" There are two basic philosophies. One extreme says that you should maintain your bike well enough that you don't need to carry tools at all. Repair it at home, not on the road. These folks just carry phone money and have Mom come get them if something really goes wrong. The other extreme carries every possible tool to fix every possible problem on every possible bike.

My rule of thumb is that you should carry the tools to get you home from any distance you are not willing to walk.

What Ten Different Types of Cyclists Carry With Them
(Adding the items as you go.)

Amy	type 1	bus money and a lock
Minimalist	type 2	patch kit, tire levers, and pump
Smart Minimalist	type 3	spare tube
Smart Cyclist	type 4	basic tool kit: tiny vise grips (5 inch)
		pocket pro "T" wrench
		3, 4, 5, 6 mm allens
		slot and Phillips screw drivers
		8, 9, 10 mm sockets
		spoke wrench; chain tool
Experienced	type 5	spare nuts, bolts and selected bearings
Touring Cyclist	type 6	spare spoke, freewheel tool, pocket vise
Smart Tourist	type 7	crankpuller, spare tire, chain lube
Traveling Tourist	type 8	pedal wrench
Good Samaritan	type 9	6, 7, and 8 above, for other kinds of bikes
Herman	type 10	big adjustable wrenches, bailing wire, and spare chain and freewheel and a rag to wipe your hands.

(Reprinted from Seattle Bicycle Atlas with permission of Carla Black and Angel Rodriguez. Angel Rodriguez produces a series of high-tech bike tools under the trade name Pocket Pro®)

First Aid

by Réanne Douglass

Several years ago on a mountain biking trip, I miscalculated a sharp turn on a sandy stretch of dirt road, went flying and turned my right shin into raw meat. I didn't have a first aid kit with me. Why bother? After all, I was cycling off-road, no traffic around, and I planned to be gone just part of the day. When I got home, I took a shower, cleaned my wound and applied some antibiotic cream. Three days later, Don had to carry me to the doctor. A staph infection – that took three pain-filled weeks to control – had set in.

Don't be careless like I was. Carry and use a First Aid Kit. You can purchase one at bike shops or sporting goods stores, or you can make your own. For starters, we suggest the following items:

8 Bandaids 1" x 3"	8 Aspirin Tablets or Aspirin Substitute
6 Antiseptic Swabs or	8 Gauze Pads 3" x 3"
1 oz. Hydrogen Peroxide	4 Antacid Tablets
1 Roll Adhesive Tape	1 Elastic Bandage
1 Moleskin 3" x 4"	1 Needle
1 Single-Edge Razor Blade	Waterproof Matches (in film can)
Sunscreen 15 SPF or more	Prescription Medicine (if applicable)

For extended overnight trips add: snake bit kit; water purification tablets; non-adhering pads 2" x 3"; insect repellent, and increase the quantities of compresses, gauze pads and bandaids.

Bicycle Clubs of the Greater San Francisco Bay Area

Most of the Pedal Tours in this book were originated by bicycle club ride leaders. If you're now hooked on Pedal Touring in our area, we suggest you contact one of these clubs and sign up for more of the same type of adventure.

Almaden Cycle Touring Club. Touring. Box 7286, San Jose, CA 95150. 408-997-9737, 408-629-2068.

Auburn Bicycle Club. Touring. 1440 Canal Street, Auburn, CA 94603. 916-885-3861.

Bay Area Roaming Tandems (BART). Tandems only. Box 2176, Los Gatos, CA 95031. 408-356-7443.

Benicia Bicycle Club. Touring, training. 707-642-6301, 707-746-0375.

Bicycle Trails Council of the East Bay. Mountain biking. Box 9583. Berkeley, CA 94709. 510-528-BIKE.

Bicycle Trails Council of Marin. Mountain biking. Box 13842, San Rafael, CA 94913. 415-472-BIKE.

Cherry City Cyclists. Touring. Box 1972, San Leandro, CA 94577.

Coast Range Riders. Mountain biking. 510-271-8004.

Davis Bicycle Club. Touring, racing. 616 Third Street, Davis, CA 95616. 916-756-3540.

Different Spokes. Recreational cycling for gays and lesbians (participation open to all). Box 14711, San Francisco, CA 94114-0711. 415-282-1647.

Eagle Cycling Club. Touring, racing. 3335 Solano Avenue, Napa, CA 94558. 707-253-7000, event line: 707-226-7066

Fremont Freewheelers. Touring, racing. Box 1069, Fremont, CA 94538. 510-797-5481.

Golden Gate Cyclists/American Youth Hostels. Touring, hosteling. 425 Divisadero, Suite 301, San Francisco, CA 94117. 415-863-9939.

Grizzly Peak Cyclists. Touring. Box 5308. Berkeley, CA 94709. 510-665-4221.

Marin Cyclists. Racing, touring. Box 2611, San Rafael, CA 94902. 415-388-3203.

Monterey Mountain Bike Association (MoMBA). Mountain biking. Box 51923, Pacific Grove, CA 93950.

Responsible Organized Mountain Pedalers (ROMP). Mountain biking. 415-941-RIDE.

Sacramento Bike Hikers. Touring. 7021 Salmon River Drive, Sacramento, CA 95842.

Sacramento Rough Riders. Mountain biking. Box 382, Sacramento, CA 95812. 916-589-1572.

Sacramento Wheelmen. Touring. 920 27th Street, Sacramento, CA 95815. 916-444-8577.

Santa Cruz County Cycling Club. Touring, racing. 414-1/2 Soquel Avenue, Santa Cruz, CA 95062. 408-423-0829.

Santa Rosa Cycling Club. Touring, racing, mountain biking. Box 11761, Santa Rosa, CA 95406.

Sausalito Cyclists. Racing, touring. 301 Calddonia, Sausalito, CA 94965. 415-332-3050.

Sierra Club, San Francisco Bay Chaper – Bicycling Section. Touring & social. 3632 Lawton, #5, San Francisco, CA 94122. 415-665-7913.

Skyline Cycling Club. Touring. Box 60126, Sunnyvale, CA 94088. 408-739-3995, 408-255-6465

Tahoe Area Mountain Bike Association (TAMBA). Mountain biking. Box 1488, Tahoe City, CA. 95730. 916-525-5100.

Valley Spokesmen Bicycle Touring Club. Racing, touring. Box 2630, Dublin, CA 94568. 510-828-5299.

Western Wheelers Bicycle Club. Touring. Box 518, Palo Alto, CA 94302. 415-858-0936.

Women's Mountain Bike & Tea Society (WOMBATS). Mountain biking for women. Box 757, Fairfax, CA 94930. 415-459-0980.

Outdoor Publications from Fine Edge Productions

Mountain Biking the High Sierra

Guide 1	Owens Valley and Inyo County, Second Edition	$8.95
Guide 2	Mammoth Lakes and Mono County, Second Edition	$8.95
Guide 3A	Lake Tahoe South, Second Edition	$8.95
Guide 3B	Lake Tahoe North, Second Edition	$8.95

Mountain Biking the Coast Range

Guide 4	Ventura County and the Sespe, Second Edition	$8.95
Guide 5	Santa Barbara County, Second Edition	$8.95
Guide 7	Santa Monica Mountains	$8.95
Guide 8	Saugus District of the Angeles N.F. with Mt. Pinos	$8.95
Guide 9	San Gabriel Mountains, Angeles N.F.	$9.95

Mountain Biking Maps (topographical)

North Lake Tahoe Basin Recreation Map, w/profiles & trail descriptions	$8.95
South Lake Tahoe Basin Recreation Map, w/profiles & trail descriptions	$8.95
San Gabriel Mountains — West; includes Verdugo Mountains	$8.95
Excelsior District, Tahoe N.F., Lake Tahoe Region, Hwy. 80	$6.95
Crystal Basin, Eldorado N.F., Lake Tahoe Region, Hwy. 50	$6.95
Moab, Utah, Slick Rock	$5.95

Also available:

Favorite Pedal Tours of Northern California	$12.95
Ski Touring the Eastern High Sierra	$8.95
Beginning and Intermediate Cross-Country Day Trips	
Exploring California's Channel Islands, an Artist's View	$6.95

Additional books and maps in process.

For current titles and prices, please send SASE.

To order any of these items see your local dealer or send
your check to Fine Edge Productions at the address below.
Please include $2.00 for shipping. California residents add sales tax.

Fine Edge Productions, Route 2, Box 303, Bishop, California 93514